HOW TO
LIVE WITH
OBJECTS

HOW TO LIVE WITH OBJECTS

A Modern Guide to More
Meaningful Interiors

Monica Khemsurov
& Jill Singer

Photographs by Charlie Schuck

Clarkson Potter/Publishers
New York

page 1 and following spread: The London home of Raphaël Zerbib

title page: The Brussels home of Hélène Rebelo and Edouard Beauget

opposite: The Rockaway Beach home of Helena Barquet and Fabiana Faria

above: Vintage planter in the Brooklyn home of Kim Mupangilaï

1: Glass flute set by Alex Brand, date unknown, courtesy of Casa Shop

2: Tubo Bookends by Bi-Rite Studio, 2019

3: Truncated tetrahedron variation vessel by Cody Hoyt, 2017

4: Orchid flower candlesticks by Sean Gerstley, 2021

5: Coffee table by Elliot Barnes in the home of Raphaël Zerbib

CONTENTS

Introduction 13
Understanding Objects 19

[→ 1] THE VINTAGE OBJECT 27
Collectors' Items 86

[→ 2] THE CONTEMPORARY OBJECT 93
Embracing Discomfort 156

[→ 3] THE HANDMADE OBJECT 163
Designer DIYs 208

[→ 4] THE SENTIMENTAL OBJECT 215
My Favorite Thing 258

[→ 5] STYLING 267

Acknowledgments 310
Photography Credits 312
Index 314

12

What is it that defines a home? Is it the perfectly chosen paint colors? The moldings, the archways, or the beams? Is it the matching nightstands, the puddled curtains, the tiled bathrooms, the oak-plank floors? For years, shelter magazines and design books defined a home that was worth having—and, by extension, a home that was worth showing off to the world—as one that was decorated just so, that paid attention to those kinds of details, and that was often brought to life by someone with professional expertise in such matters. And while those homes were often beautiful, they sometimes evoked an uneasy sense of anonymity; you got the same feeling from looking at them as you did from flipping through the catalog of a big-box furniture store. You wondered, "Who, exactly, lives here?"

When we founded our online magazine Sight Unseen more than a decade ago—with the mission to provide readers with a highly personal look at design objects and the creative people behind them—we made a conscious decision to approach interiors from a radically different point of view. We believed, and still do, that while layout and fixtures and fabrics can all play a part in making a space aesthetically pleasing, it's the objects you surround yourself with that truly give your home its soul: the vintage Danish chair you found at a flea market, the indigo vase you bought from an LA ceramicist, the candlesticks a friend brought back from Mexico, the side table you've been saving up to buy from a designer you follow on Instagram. These objects are the story you tell to the world about your personality and your obsessions, your experiences and your memories, your desires and your intentions. Infused with your personal narrative, they provide a catalyst for conversation when friends visit (or virtually view) your home, and a comfort for when you're cooped up inside, as so many of us were in recent years.

At the start of 2020, three weeks into quarantine, we got an email from a literary agent in New York asking if we might be interested in writing a book; stuck at home, people were looking for inspiration and new ways to think about their interiors. A Sight Unseen book was something we'd thought about—and been asked about—for years, but had never pursued, partly because the idea of putting together a compendium of our past stories, or our favorite homes and design studios, never really felt momentous enough to us. But the pandemic brought us a whole new perspective. When we thought about what we were collectively going through at the time, and how our objects were such a huge source of comfort in isolation, it became clear that we had to write *this* book: *How to Live with Objects*, a comprehensive guide to incorporating meaningful works of art and design into your home. The book would be expansive enough that its ideas could remain relevant for years to come, and it would allow us to combine all of our interests, and everything we'd learned over the course of our careers, into a single volume. The idea that you should accumulate, not decorate. The idea that opposing forces, like contemporary and vintage, ought to live in harmony in your space. The idea that it's okay to think about your home not as something to be completed, but as a forever work in progress, in the same way that you yourself probably are. Plus, everything you've always wanted to know about objects: why they're important, who makes them, what makes them valuable, how to acquire them, and, ultimately, how to put them together in a way that's warm, inviting, and extremely personal— without a hefty budget or the help of an interior designer or decorator.

These ideas have always felt personal to us, because it was objects that paved the way for our interest in design. Neither of us studied design in school—we're both trained as journalists— but both of us had formative experiences with design by way of the domestic items we grew up with. When Jill looks back on her suburban Midwestern childhood, she remembers the tulip-patterned Marimekko sheets, the wooden highboy engraved with yellow flowers, the lamp depicting a unicorn resting in a garden, and the sofa embroidered with tropical florals. Monica, growing up in Ohio, actually lived with some design classics, like Breuer's Cesca and Wassily chairs. But as a lover of all things colorful and sparkly, her bedroom as a five-year-old consisted of wild Memphis-style sheets and a funny collection of Swarovski crystal animals that her dad brought her each time he came home from a work trip. These objects remain firmly implanted in our memories and represent the first time we experienced a strong emotional connection to our physical environment.

As a child, when you live with things someone else has chosen for you, you either don't feel anything for them at all or you ascribe meaning to them via your imagination. Things also tend to hold more meaning when they act as your introduction to something, which is why your favorite album is often the first one you heard by that band, or why your first love sticks with you for so long. As you grow older, it's important to keep intact the magic of those childhood things. If you can choose your objects with care, educating yourself about where they came from and making the experience of acquiring them part of the story—rather than, say, throwing a bunch of stuff into your cart as you browse a Target late at night—your relationship to objects can become exponentially more meaningful as you age.

At its core, that's what this book is about, and it's an idea we've been exploring ever since we founded Sight

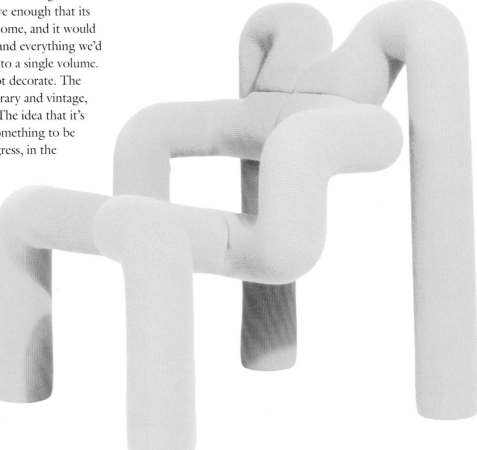

Ekstrem Chair by Terje Ekstrøm for Varier Furniture, designed in 1972 and produced in 1984

Unseen. In the early days, when we would visit one of our creative friends for the site's popular At Home With column, we focused on objects partly out of necessity. We often couldn't afford a photographer, and we weren't adept enough image-makers to create the kind of perfect sweeping room views readers want to see in their home tours. But we were also inherently more interested in our subjects' possessions than in how well coordinated their living rooms were. We'd ask them to show us their favorite books, or tell us more about the objects on their shelves that may have played a part in inspiring their work. We'd beg for the history behind architect Rafael de Cardenas's vintage Ikea chair, or ask to peek inside the pages of creative director Joseph Magliaro's Alessandro Mendini–designed *Casabella* magazines. The goal of Sight Unseen has always been to tell the stories behind the stuff—both the things people have made and the things they've acquired—and that always felt like the best way to understand our subjects on a deeper level. Objects were the perfect conduit for our storytelling.

At the time of Sight Unseen's founding in 2009, we were one of the only publications doing the work of demystifying the world of design for people outside the industry and focusing on the importance of objects and how they're made. Design was still a niche interest when we started, one much lower on the totem pole of cultural relevance than fashion or art. Our friends working in those industries didn't pay too much attention to what we were doing, nor did they really seem to understand it. But over the past decade, we've watched the world tilt in our direction. Provenance—the idea that knowing where something came from makes it inherently more valuable—was always a thing in the vintage furniture market, but it was around that time that people started to truly be interested in throwing back the curtain on all of the possessions they sought to acquire. This curiosity had its roots in the slow food movement, but it soon expanded to areas

such as beauty, fashion, and contemporary design, with a raft of online magazines suddenly popping up to interrogate the building blocks of our closets, our medicine cabinets, and our domestic spaces.

It was probably social media, though, that created a perfect storm in terms of accelerating the personal style revolution and the ascendancy of design in popular culture. Instagram debuted not even a year after we started Sight Unseen, and people began obsessively documenting the world around them, then turned their cameras on their own homes. Social media is how a six-foot-tall, neon-pink Ettore Sottsass mirror went from being a luxury reserved for people like Karl Lagerfeld to a selfie spot at New York's Opening Ceremony to the ultimate influencer accessory (and subject of a 2019 *New York* magazine profile). It's how terrazzo took over the world, as people began posting photos of the floors beneath them on their travels, a look that soon translated into housewares and accessories. It's how a series of previously under-the-radar archival chair designs—ranging from Mario Botta's metal rollback Seconda to the spidery '80s-era Ekstrem to Herman Miller's gum-inspired Chiclet—became status symbols and household names. "To own one was to buy a new kind of social media bragging rights—a sign of in-the-know sophistication," the fashion trade magazine *WWD* wrote about the phenomenon.

Since then, design has gained an unprecedented level of mass appeal, with personal narrative becoming a driving force in decorating. Where once you showed off your outfit of the day, now you might document your morning matcha ritual, complete with a locally made mug and a vintage wooden French milking stool (a typology that was itself the subject of a mocking SSENSE article back in 2020 on "the misplaced virtue of endlessly curating corners with handmade objects"). Where once interior designers focused exclusively on expensive antiques and twentieth-century icons like Jean Prouvé and

Seconda Armchairs by Mario Botta for Alias, 1982, courtesy of Rago/Wright

Charlotte Perriand, now they fill their clients' homes with increasingly obscure contemporary pieces scouted from design stores and galleries, or fairs like our own Sight Unseen Offsite, which gives emerging designers a platform through which to show and sell their work. Design has also seeped into more and more categories of the home—we're talking toilet brushes, menorahs, and bongs here—enabling more people than ever before to acquire something beautiful or unique.

The current moment has added yet another, unforeseen element to the equation. Like social media before it, virtual work-from-home apps such as Zoom have made everyone's private lives and spaces even more public than they were before, giving rise to a new brand of voyeurism—what the *New York Times* calls "décor peeping." That's not going to change anytime soon, as working from your sofa has become the new normal. As a result, curating your home, and the objects you surround yourself with, has taken on even greater importance.

In the following pages, we'll be introducing four different categories of objects—vintage, contemporary, handmade, and sentimental—and guiding you through the process of identifying good ones, as well as explaining where to find them and how to incorporate them into your space. If you're new to collecting, this book will teach you how to

find and identify makers and styles you love, which questions to ask when purchasing objects, the secret tactics vintage collectors and interior designers use when shopping online, and why it's okay to have at least one thing in your home that no one else understands. If you're a creative person for whom living with objects is already second nature, this book will provide inspiration in the form of incredible interiors, styling tutorials, and conversations with collectors, designers, curators, stylists, and more.

Of course, there have been books before ours that take a categorical approach to the foundations of a home. One of the most iconic examples—and a huge inspiration for this book—is 1974's *The House Book* by Terence Conran. It's a touchstone in the design community both for its time-capsule interior photographs and its granular look at different interior styles, layouts, and elements, from heating to hi-fi systems. Part of the fun of that book is the sheer abundance of its information; it could practically stand in for a more formal introductory design education. But *How to Live with Objects* is the first book of its kind to focus on a more universal and relevant theme: Not everyone who hunts down a copy of *The House Book* is planning to change out their window treatments, but every single person who picks up *How to Live with Objects* is a collector of things, and our book's contents will help you refine your collection, no matter what journey you're on.

left: Vilbert Chair by Verner Panton for Ikea, 1993, courtesy of BILLY.forsale
right: Plump Side Table by Ian Alistair Cochran, 2019

Coffee table by Kathryn Bentley and sculpture by Peter Shire in the LA home of Kathryn Bentley

18

Basis Chair by Falke Svatun, 2020

UNDER–
STANDING
OBJECTS

19

Many years ago, we interviewed the respected Minnesota furniture designer Jonathan Muecke, who got his start making enigmatic room dividers and minimal, abstract pieces that didn't have any immediately obvious function. He explained to us that, in fact, his work did indeed have a function: to exert a palpable influence on the energy in a room. That powerful idea has stuck with us ever since. From our chairs to our vases to the souvenirs brought back from our travels, the objects we choose to live with aren't merely nice to look at; they can significantly affect the mood of a room and its occupants. Imbued with the stories of where they came from and why we chose them, our objects radiate meaning into our space, triggering us to remember, feel, or think while giving our guests a tangible sense of our personality. More than any other element of our interiors, they are what make our homes definitively ours.

Indeed, as we noted in the introduction, the premise at the heart of our book is that the objects we surround ourselves with are so much more important and relevant than the overall "design" of our living spaces, which means that you don't have to be a decorator or an expert or a rich person to achieve the perfect object-filled home. For many people, it might be new or unusual to think about interiors like this—as driven more by our personal possessions than by our decorating prowess—but we've felt that way for as long as we've been design editors, and it's been a core principle of Sight Unseen's coverage since we began the site in 2009. We figured it would be useful, with this section, to take a moment to elucidate our approach to objects before taking a closer look at the objects themselves.

WHAT IS AN OBJECT?

First things first: We should probably define what exactly counts as an "object." For our purposes, it's something that's three-dimensional rather than two-dimensional. And while larger furniture pieces such as beds and sofas may occasionally be included, we'll be primarily focusing on smaller items that are easier to acquire, and that are among the typologies more typically addressed by contemporary makers. An object, in our sense of the word, may be anonymous or by someone well known, and can be rustic and crafty or highly refined and sculptural, but it always holds some sort of aesthetic appeal, and is always at least one step above the merely utilitarian. So, it's not the TV remote or the microwave, but rather your favorite thrift-store mug, or the bookends your parents got as a wedding present that you've requisitioned for yourself, or the 1960s Italian table lamp you coveted for ages before scoring one online.

Can an artwork be an object? Yes, especially in the sense that artists make functional pieces like vases or plates from time to time. There's also quite a bit of overlap between the design and art realms when it comes to sculptural forms that don't have a specific function, but have an object-like feel. That said,

you'll find that most of the objects in this book are by people who identify themselves as designers rather than artists, with the distinction often being that the process of making—with its attention to materials, techniques, shapes, and details—is more important to their practice than an overarching concept or narrative.

Part of understanding what counts as an object is understanding what counts as a good object. The obvious answer is that a good object is one that moves you or is important to you. But for the times when you can't quite decide, we can share a little trick we use whenever we're determining whether to acquire an item or feature it on our website: We ask ourselves whether it's "well-resolved," which means whether it's a good idea, well executed, that has no design features we would want to add or take away. That's our secret, make-or-break equation for determining whether we fundamentally like something. Because we're design editors who pass judgment on objects every day, the process happens near-instantaneously in our minds, but it's easy to learn and is a great starting point for evaluating the worthiness of the pieces you might invite into your life.

One thing that definitely does *not* determine whether an object is good is how much it costs, or how much it's worth. The objects we love, and the objects in this book, span all conceivable price ranges, from zero to six figures. Think about the amazing drinking glasses you found at a garage sale for $1, or the ceramic box your friend made you—sometimes the things we spend the least on have more value to us than our splurges. Breaking down that more abstract sense of value is our next step.

WHY WE LIVE WITH OBJECTS

We don't really need to persuade anyone to live with objects, of course, because most who are fortunate enough to have a stable dwelling already do it without thinking. Living with objects we care about—for reasons that transcend their basic function—is something that has always come naturally to humans, whether those things are items we've kept as reminders of the past or are new ones we've acquired to please our eyes as our tastes and interests change. Objects are an important part of our personal emotional landscape in so many ways. Here are three of them.

Objects make us feel

We tend to think of objects as being either active or passive. Passive objects are ones that simply exist in the background of our lives, sitting there unnoticed until we need to use them. Most of them are merely utilitarian, as we mentioned above, but even a decorative vase can be passive if it means absolutely nothing to you; maybe you got it with your last flower delivery, and it's so generic you keep it buried in the back of a cupboard. Active objects, on the other hand, have an (ideally positive) energy that activates certain feelings or thoughts inside us. Sometimes they bring up good memories of a person, a place, or a time in our lives. Sometimes they fill us with curiosity, or remind us that someone cares about us. Sometimes they simply bring us emotional comfort, making us feel cozy and secure in a space that feels uniquely ours—and maybe making us feel less alone. "If you invite a few objects into your house, it's the same as inviting a few people over," says the Berlin-based design curator Matylda Krzykowski. "Who do you want to be surrounded by? What do they bring to your life? Objects all have a different shape, character, and aura, and they become inhabitants of your surroundings, along with you."

Objects tell stories

We started Sight Unseen because as journalists, we particularly loved telling the stories behind the designs we admired, and the stories of the designers who made them. When it comes to actually living with those objects, though, it isn't necessarily the narratives belonging to their creators that we find most compelling, but rather the ones we ourselves begin building around those objects the moment they enter our lives. That includes stories about the amazing lengths we've gone to in order to get something we particularly coveted, or stories about how a loved one surprised us with a particular piece as a gift. Our objects can carry family histories as they're passed down through generations, or just remind us of a really nice day we spent in a particular place. Objects also help us build connections with others, acting as the catalyst that inspires us to tell them those stories. And the mystery of wanting to know more about objects can draw us in deeper to people or places, helping us get to know them better. Whenever she walks into a new environment, the first thing Krzykowski does is "scan every object in the space," she says. "I'm looking at the bowl that's shaped like cabbage, or a beautiful blue fly swatter, asking myself, was it a gift? Was it bought in a secondhand store? How did it get here?"

Objects reflect us

"My house is not 'just a thing,'" wrote communications professor Dr. Karen Lollar in 2010, in her research about what happens when we lose our home to a fire. "It's not merely a possession or a structure of unfeeling walls. It's an extension of my physical body and my sense of self that reflects who I was, am, and want to be." The same sentiment applies to the objects our homes contain: In 1988, a researcher named Russell W. Belk wrote a seminal paper coining the term "extended self," which refers to the belongings we surround

Cork lamp by Ingo Maurer and Wilhelm Zanoth, 1974, courtesy of Béton Brut

ourselves with that we see as physical manifestations of our identity and our personal style. Brands have been marketing to us based on that tendency for decades because most of us really do place extremely high value on what our objects project about us to the outside world. It may sound a bit shallow until you consider that we're social animals, and anything that helps us relate to others can serve an important purpose in our lives. When someone walks into your home and sees the items you live with, they may start to understand you better, and they may even see commonalities between your interests and their own, bringing you closer together. Your objects can establish your identity and your tribe not only publically—on social media, for example—but within your private relationships, too.

To truly comprehend why these three elements make it so fulfilling to live with objects, all you need to do is imagine your home completely emptied of them: It would be missing so much curiosity, connection, and personality—missing so much joy, really. Fortunately, it's a scenario we're here to help you avoid!

HOW TO LIVE WITH OBJECTS

The thing about living with objects is that there's no one right way to live with objects. The whole point of approaching your home this way is to make it as personal as possible, so you can live in a space that represents *you* and engages *you*—the goal being to keep the process genuine and to have fun while you're doing it. Of course we all want our interiors to look good, and of course it's important to be mindful of sustainability and only buy the things you plan to live with for a while, so to that end we definitely have a lot of actionable advice for you in the coming chapters. But really almost anyone can do this.

You don't need to be a decorator

As we mentioned above, you don't have to have any special decorating skills to improve your home by taking a thoughtful approach to objects, or to benefit from the ideas and advice in this book. To clarify what we mean by that, decorating is the art of curating and orchestrating the elements of a room in the most layered, balanced, and visually pleasing way in order to achieve an overarching artistic vision. In decorating, the vision is the star. In this book, the individual objects are the star, and the main gratification isn't in coordinating them in some impressive way but in simply acquiring and appreciating them. When you buy a weird, multicolor extruded-plastic toilet-paper holder by the London designer James Shaw, for example, you aren't doing so because you've found the perfect match for your sink hardware, but because you've fallen in love with something that's totally unique, created by someone interesting, and capable of delighting you every time you enter the bathroom. "I think the best interiors are less contrived and more emotionally driven—more about how they make you feel than how they look," says Alex Gilbert, associate director of the Friedman Benda gallery in New York. "Our apartment isn't designed; it's just an assemblage of things we like. For someone who's just getting into this, that feels less intimidating than 'I need to draw up a floor plan and figure out every single object.'"

This is a relatively novel idea—especially coming from a high-end design expert—that reflects the way we live now. Of course, some people still hire decorators to source their objects and coordinate their rugs with their window treatments, in the vein of famous bygone icons like Jean-Michel Frank, Albert Hadley, or Sister Parish. But these days if you ask a design lover to name a great interior, they're just as likely to reference the eclectic apartment of a random creative they follow on Instagram as they are to choose a perfectly appointed, rarity-filled penthouse by a famous designer. The spaces that get respect now are the ones that have the best things—a ceramic Eny Lee Parker lamp, a 1970s Rodolfo Bonetto Melaina chair, unusual planters scored at a flea market—and if they're in no apparent order, it's not really a deal breaker anymore. John Meyers, one half of the soap-making duo Wary Meyers, who are known on social media for their savage garage-saleing skills, is a good example of this mentality: "In our dining room now, there are paintings and prints leaning against the wall, stacks of ice buckets, and an inflatable banana," he says. "It may not make sense to anyone, but it makes sense to me— these things make me happy."

That said, we do think that living with objects is even more enjoyable when some attention has been paid to their context and their arrangement, and you'll find no shortage of inspiration in the interiors dotted throughout the following chapters. But this can be as simple as juxtaposing objects made from different materials and textures on a shelf, or highlighting

Nebula Alpha bong by Serena Confalonieri, 2021

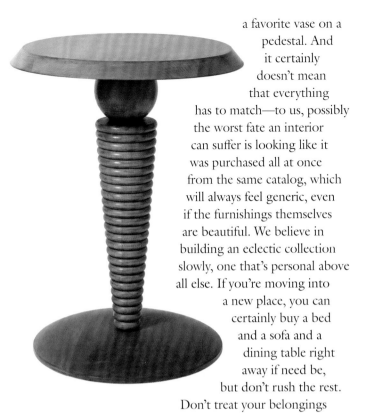

a favorite vase on a pedestal. And it certainly doesn't mean that everything has to match—to us, possibly the worst fate an interior can suffer is looking like it was purchased all at once from the same catalog, which will always feel generic, even if the furnishings themselves are beautiful. We believe in building an eclectic collection slowly, one that's personal above all else. If you're moving into a new place, you can certainly buy a bed and a sofa and a dining table right away if need be, but don't rush the rest. Don't treat your belongings like a shopping list. As Catherine Lock, creative director of the British luxury handmade goods retailer The New Craftsmen, once told the blog The Modern House, "I'm always amazed when I see these homes that come together in an instant, because I wonder how much they express their owner's style. Homemaking is done bit-by-bit, in a process that you form and layer with your own aesthetic over time."

You don't need to be a collector

As for the idea of "collecting," our thoughts on this are similar to our thoughts on "decorating": You also don't have to aspire to be a collector in the traditional sense of the word, with its connotations of spending a fortune on museum-quality pieces. You just need to buy what you love, trust your instincts, and understand the power of having these objects in your life. Even some of our favorite big-name collectors from the past—who *did* own museum-quality art and design—displayed their least-expensive finds right alongside their most-expensive ones, drawing intriguing visual parallels between them while conveying that true beauty transcends provenance and typology. The late chemist Dr. Albert C. Barnes, whose vast trove of art and objects has its own museum in Philadelphia, collected everything from Native American pottery to Matisse masterworks to everyday objects, including 887 pieces of wrought iron; he arranged them into narrative vignettes he called "ensembles," where a Picasso might hang next to a spatula or a yarn spinner. The late British art curator Jim Ede had a similar approach, devoting equal attention and space in his home to pieces by Brâncuși and Max Ernst as he did to handmade chairs, rock collections, driftwood, broom heads, and textiles. Had someone replaced the priceless artworks in both collections with equally beautiful but anonymous ones, neither would feel less impactful.

You don't need a perfect house

One common denominator among many of the homes featured in shelter magazines such as *Architectural Digest* or *Elle Décor* is that they're ambitiously renovated, and often owned rather than rented—those are the kinds of spaces that have traditionally been held up as aspirational when it comes to interior design, and for many of us they're so out of reach that it's hard to relate. But as we noted in the introduction, in our object-oriented world, where you live is infinitely less important than how you live. Monica, for example, rents a 500-square-foot apartment in a 220-year-old Brooklyn rowhouse with cracking walls, crooked floors, and ancient windowsills that never really look clean; as a collector of objects, though, her colorful finds distract from the imperfections of her place and tell a story that's wholly independent of them. Plus, if you do live in a rental and can't make architectural changes to it, shifting your focus to objects gives you the opportunity to put your stamp on your space in a meaningful way.

You don't need to be a maximalist

Even if you're a minimalist, you can—and should—surround yourself with objects. You just have to make a bigger impact with fewer of them. So many tastemakers have proven this in their own spaces, including the Sydney interior designer Olivia Bossy, whose home is a Zen-like, clutter-free homage to beige yet is punctuated sparsely and intentionally with handmade ceramics, curiosities like an ostrich egg on a stand, and sculptural vintage lamps. Those are the pieces that instantly telegraph her taste, not to mention give her home a warmth and humanity it might otherwise be lacking. "This idea of bare white walls and a wooden floor that stems from the Modernism ideology, I'm against it, because it encourages us to all live the same way," says Krzykowski. "It's not conducive to originality. Living with objects helps you define an identity. At the end, it's the objects that create an environment."

26

Anthroposophical chair, circa 1930, courtesy of Béton Brut

THE VINTAGE OBJECT

27

If we had to rank the most incredible feelings that human beings are capable of experiencing, at the top of our list would be all the obvious ones, like falling in love, eating an amazing meal, or singing karaoke. But right up there with the best of them would be a more obscure but equally powerful rush: the one we get wading through a sea of generic junk at a flea market or on eBay, when suddenly we spot an object that's exactly right—something so different and wonderful that our adrenaline starts flowing and we feel giddy and electrified, as though we've just won some cosmic lottery. When we asked famed interior designer Kelly Wearstler to describe that same feeling, she called it "profound" and says she refers to it as "a beautiful addiction," one she's had herself since she was a girl going to yard sales with her mom. The obsession with hunting for amazing vintage objects is a process that makes whatever treasure you do find seem a million times more personal, almost like it found you. It's pure gratification.

We've thought a lot about why the highs of vintage shopping are so intense (and the lows, for that matter, when you miss out on something you want). It's all wrapped up in what makes vintage objects so particularly special. All of the best ones are rare, and finding them isn't easy. It requires work, it requires luck, and it requires being able to identify what's good when you find it—what most people would call "having an eye." So when you do come across that perfect thing, it feels like a personal achievement: Even if that 1940s candlestick or Postmodern vase wasn't one-of-a-kind when it was made, it might as well be now, and to have found and chosen something so obscure serves as certified proof of your refined taste. The late, great *Vogue* editor Diana Vreeland may have put it best when she famously said "Style—all who have it share one thing: originality." While she was referring primarily to her own realm, fashion, the same is definitely true of interiors—all of the great ones have a strong personality, and when it comes to making a space feel singular, there's nothing quite as effective as vintage.

Why vintage now?

It's no coincidence that we're living in a time when people are especially fanatical about surrounding themselves with bygone objects. As we discussed earlier in this book, our homes are on public display in truly unprecedented ways—thanks to the voyeuristic nature of social media and the shift to at-home video calling—and because most goods are now mass-manufactured in huge numbers, there's social currency in owning something really different. That said, throughout history, there has always been some form of value placed on the unique. Ancient kings and aristocrats, while their interiors weren't intended to defy any stylistic expectations, did indulge in the privilege of having bespoke furnishings made for them by highly skilled artisans—pieces that were so well constructed, they could be passed down to future generations. Those antiques were cherished not because they were obscure, though, but because they were family heirlooms, representing the exquisite trappings of extreme wealth.

In the nineteenth century, with the rise of the antiques trade in Paris, acquiring old furniture became about collecting rather than simply inheriting, but still typically entailed spending a lot of money on very high-end, finely crafted items that could fit into a period-specific room or home.

That started to change a bit in the twentieth century with the rise of eclecticism, as decorators like Billy Baldwin, Tony Duquette, and Sister Parish began breaking up the homogeneity of their interiors with more unusual, incongruous objects, setting the stage for how we use vintage furnishings today. Vreeland's decorator George Stacey, for example, famously installed two inexpensive picnic chairs amid all the pricey antiques in her Park Avenue apartment. Of course back then, being a middle-class person with more pedestrian hand-me-downs—especially if they were less than a hundred years old, in line with what we'd consider "vintage" now—was not very chic, unless you were a French New Wave character, or Patti Smith, and it was part of your glamorous starving-artist vibe. These days we look at preloved objects quite differently, and appreciate them for different reasons.

A mystery and a history

Compared to what you'd buy brand-new, a vintage object has the added dimension of a past, and the contrast between the two worlds is greater now than it's ever been. A vintage object asks you to consider questions like: How did this thing come to be? Who made it? What lives did it live before I found it? As the New York design dealer Patrick Parrish put it when we interviewed him for this book, "Vintage has a mystery and a history." Even if you don't know the story behind that old ceramic sculpture, you can invent one; even if you don't know who owned your Eames chair before you did, you can imagine all the possibilities. When vintage furnishings are visibly weathered—with what professionals would call "a patina"—those stories become even more evident and compelling. It lends vintage objects an intriguing aura that newly manufactured ones just don't have, which in turn adds a palpable warmth to your home. "You have your shiny new

L'Oeil Floor Lamp by Nicola L, 1966, in the home of Yoram Heller and Eleanor Wells

things, and your old things that have an age and a weight, and each makes the other look better," says Helena Barquet, cofounder of the New York design store Coming Soon. "I think most people live with that mix."

Unlike traditional heirloom antiques, vintage objects also offer modern shoppers incredible value—their rise might be the greatest design democratizer of our time. That's because when you're buying new objects, the price you pay almost always reflects a mark-up on the actual cost of materials and labor, which can be anywhere from 100 to 500 percent. But when you're buying vintage objects, the price simply represents a negotiation between how much the seller wants and how much the customer is willing to pay. So unless you're among the tiny minority of collectors fighting over Prouvé chairs at Design Miami, you can usually get a high-quality, well-made vintage piece for far less than you'd pay for a brand-new but poorly made one. Case in point: Monica's own beloved leather sectional sofa, which was made by a respected Italian brand in the '70s, and had a luxury price tag at the time, but which she purchased for $900 from an aunt of hers who wanted something new. There's no way a brand-new $900 sofa would hold up through more than half a century of use.

Even if you can't find a screaming deal like that one, though, vintage furniture's typically low cost-to-quality ratio fills a hole in the market created by the very nature of contemporary global production—one that anyone who's actually tried to shop for a sofa on a budget is likely already familiar with. On one hand, you have the handmade designer object that's impeccably crafted but wildly expensive; on the other, the object that's made in a factory, and therefore subject to huge order minimums, which retailers can only profit from by driving down costs. There's really no feasible production method in between the two, so vintage has become the primary option for so-called affordable luxury, which is exactly why increasingly design-savvy young people have become so obsessed with it. They're even using vintage objects as more affordable stand-ins for art: Instead of a $5,000 sculpture on the mantel, it's $5 sculptural candlesticks from the thrift store. The visual statement is no less impactful.

Permission to let loose

For those of us who are a bit older, our love of vintage is often bound up in nostalgia for items or aesthetics we grew up around. The colorful, Marimekko-esque graphic bed sheets, the all-beige living rooms, the floral upholstery—these memories come back to us as we age, and we often find ourselves gravitating toward them again, triggering eras of design to cycle back into style the same way they do in fashion. But just like in fashion, even those who haven't lived through an era can become transfixed by it—otherwise, how could 20-somethings have gone through such an intense period of longing for everything from the '80s movement known as Memphis? While it's always wise to invest in pieces you think you'll feel connected to over the long run, part of the fun of buying vintage is that you can try these kinds of trends on for size without fear of making a mistake. The very nature of vintage makes it more permissible to let loose: You can take huge aesthetic risks on an object when you're buying it for cheap at a flea market. Barquet told us that vintage purchases give her license to be "a little more tacky, a little more fun. The weirder the better—it shows you have a point of view."

If that ruffled '80s sofa doesn't end up working out in your interior, or if you grow tired of it over time, the beauty of vintage is that you can sell it, donate it, or, worst-case scenario, throw it away knowing that you technically didn't waste any resources by purchasing it in the first place. Buying vintage is essentially recycling, and in this age of climate change and prioritizing sustainability, there's great satisfaction in taking someone else's unwanted item and giving it a new life, a process we will attempt to demystify in the remainder of this chapter.

Of course, there are some people who think living with someone else's used furniture is gross. But to them we say: Just how often are you planning to lick it?

Vintage painted tile coffee table, date unknown, courtesy of Cupio Gallery & 1stDibs

above left: Wooden pitcher, date
unknown, courtesy of Casa Shop

above: Vintage Murano glass vase,
courtesy of Jean-Marc Fray Antiques
& 1stDibs

left: Relief of nose of Michaelangelo's
David, 1990s, from the collection of
Sadie Perry

opposite: Nude sculpture signed
by E. Valat, 1999, courtesy of The
Peanut Vendor

above: XUM flatware by Robert Wilhite
for Bissell & Wilhite, 1990, courtesy of
Casa Shop

right: Bandiera desk by Alessandro
Mendini for Tribu Editions, 1988,
courtesy of A1043

INSPIRATION

Before we dive deep into the world of vintage shopping, we need to make one thing clear: You don't need any specialized knowledge to collect vintage. You don't need to be able to identify the history of every object you find at a flea market or antique mall—especially because the dealers have often done it for you, and Google can do the rest. You don't even need to know what you're looking for, or how much it's worth when you find it. Unless you're planning on dealing vintage yourself, or making an investment in a really expensive piece, your only job is to seek out the objects you instinctively feel a connection to. Believe us when we say that we've been writing about design for almost twenty years, and we don't know even a tiny fraction of what a professional like Patrick Parrish knows. If we're able to buy vintage confidently, it's only because we pay attention when we're out there looking, we know what we like, and we refuse to let anything intimidate us.

Almost everything we do know about vintage, we learned from shopping. Shopping as much as possible—even if you don't buy anything, which we don't 99.9 percent of the time—is the single best thing you can do to improve your vintage game. That's because the more you see what's out there, the more you start to build a mental catalog of the eras, styles, and designers you're most interested in, which is the foundation from which all of your collecting decisions should be made. There are so many places to find inspiration, whether you're out walking the famous Brimfield Antique Flea Market in Massachusetts or just browsing eBay at home in your pajamas. You can mine those experiences for information, and over time it really adds up.

The best place to hone your eye these days is probably online. And the beauty of online shopping is that you don't even need to know where to look! You just need to give yourself time to get lost in a wormhole, which is where all of the best discoveries happen. Whenever we're bored, we hop on to one of the big vintage sites—like eBay, Etsy, 1stDibs, Chairish, or LiveAuctioneers—and we start by searching for whatever pops into our head that day. It could be as specific as "Vetri Murano glass pencil lamp" or as generic as "vintage marble table." Then we comb through the results, being sure to check out any related pieces that are linked, and sometimes starting new searches using whatever names or details came up in the process. Wormholes are also your friend on Instagram; if you search "vintage" on the discover page and find a seller whose pieces look interesting, you can use the "Suggested for

you" function on their profile page to follow similar accounts. Then you've got a daily inspiration feed at your fingertips.

Here's the key to all of this, though: When something catches your eye while you're browsing, take a minute to look closely at it and decipher exactly what it is you like about it. Is it the shape? The material? The texture? The color? The particular way the legs on a chair curve out at an interesting angle? Make a mental note of that information, and preserve it by saving the piece to a desktop folder or a Pinterest account, which will help you build a library of references (and search terms) to shop with later. And if the piece is attributed to a known designer, era, manufacturer, or movement, note that, too. Better yet, buy a book about it, which will likely feature archival examples of work that you'd never even find on the Internet. Before you know it, you'll be telling people how much you love Gerald Summers chairs or Elsa Peretti boxes, and maybe even spotting one for sale somewhere.

It was an Instagram wormhole, for example, that introduced us to the work of the mid-century Swedish designer Axel Einar Hjorth—whose chunky wooden furniture features delightfully curved and scalloped silhouettes—opening our eyes to our enjoyment of the Swedish Grace movement, of which he was a part. We thought we'd take a moment here to share some of our other favorite designers and movements from the past, in case it helps inspire your own vintage journey. If you read Sight Unseen, you'll know that some of our interests wax and wane as certain trends rise and fall, but these are among the stalwarts that have persisted.

● WIENER WERKSTÄTTE [→ 1]

We love the strong, graphic lines and grids of Austro-Hungarian designer Josef Hoffmann, and the work that came out of the influential decorative arts society he founded with Koloman Moser in 1903.

● BRUTALISM [→ 2]

Some people find the geometric, concrete-heavy works of the 1950s Brutalist movement cold and oppressive, but we find them groundbreaking and visually fascinating.

● INSPIRATIONAL WOMEN [→ 3]

Some of our favorite influential twentieth-century designers were women, including Cini Boeri, Eileen Gray, Gabriella Crespi, Afra Scarpa, Gae Aulenti, and Anni Albers. Many of them didn't get the recognition they deserved at the time, their legacies overshadowed by their male peers. Luckily, in recent years, that's changed a lot.

● CROSS-DISCIPLINARIANS [→ 4]

As editors, we've always had a particular fascination with the perspectives of creatives who practice across multiple mediums, from fine art to design to architecture. Some of the historical examples we admire most include Francis Bacon, Méret Oppenheim, Roberto Burle Marx, Alexander Calder, and Marianne Brandt.

● EVERYTHING ITALIAN [→ 5]

Brazil, Scandinavia, and even the United States helped define the evolution of design in the twentieth century, but Italy's contribution holds the most special place in our hearts, from brands like Saporiti and Flos, to designers like Gio Ponti and Vico Magistretti, to buildings like Villa Necchi Campiglio and the Brion Cemetery, to movements like Memphis and Radical Architecture.

Once you know you really love a movement like Brutalism, for example, or the work of female Italian designers, even if you can't afford the original objects made in that period or by those people, you can use those touchpoints as mood boards, figuratively speaking, for whatever objects are within your reach. We love snooping flea markets for pieces that somehow seem to fit certain schools of thought, even if they were made by someone completely anonymous—it's often more fun than acquiring the real thing, because it's more of a challenge.

We didn't go to school to study design history, and we still have so much to learn. But the bottom line is that the more you look at historical objects, the more you become mindful of what you're drawn toward. That's how you start to define or refine your own taste.

1: Basket by Josef Hoffmann for Wiener Werkstätte, 1905

2: Argente cabinet by Paul Evans for Directional, 1968

3: Collage rug by Eileen Gray for Ecart International, produced in 1978

4: Light by Alexander Calder, c. 1960

5: Coffee table by Massimo Vignelli, c. 1985

All courtesy of Rago/Wright

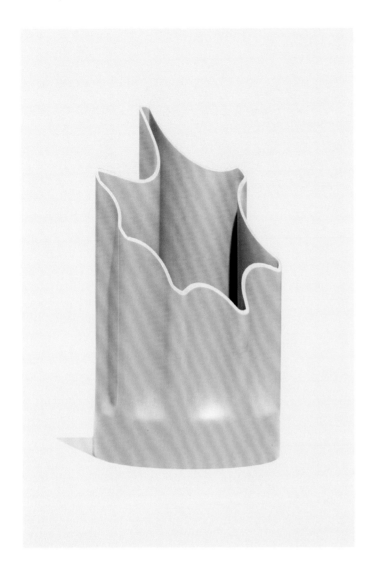

above left: Bambu vase, Model 3084D, by Enzo Mari for Danese, 1969, courtesy of Rago/Wright

above right: Italian amber glass candelabra, date unknown, courtesy of Casa Shop

right: Incamiciato vase by Murano, c. 1930, courtesy of Rago/Wright

opposite: Carved pine side tables, 1980s, courtesy of M. Kardana

SHOPPING

Once you're ready to shop for acquisition rather than inspiration, you've entered the realm of what vintage professionals affectionately call "the hunt." It's a very intentional word choice, referencing not only the adrenaline rush we talked about earlier, and the triumph of finally capturing your prize, but the primary focus placed on the process itself. Patrick Parrish, who wrote a great book called *The Hunt* in 2018 about his experiences and advice dealing vintage, puts it this way: "For collectors, once they've found something, it goes on a shelf and they don't think about it again. Looking for it is the important part."

The hunt has changed a lot in the past decade. For the non-professional, shopping for vintage used to take a lot of time and practice, from finding and attending local auctions to taking repeated trips to the antique mall. Beginning that journey used to be "a daunting experience," says Kelly Wearstler, who certainly would know—she's bought so much vintage in her twenty-five-year career that she keeps a 15,000-square-foot storage space to hold it all. "But with all these websites," she says, "it's so much more accessible now." And not only do big marketplace sites like 1stDibs and eBay offer far more of us the ability to easily do our own vintage hunting from home, Instagram in the past few years has opened the

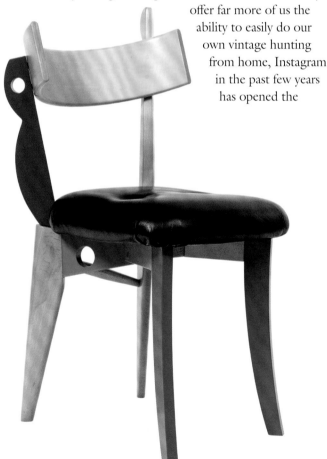

floodgates to new dealers, who are out there doing all of the shopping for us. All we have to do is sit back and watch the highly curated stream of objects flow by.

That said, the meteoric rise of Instagram accounts selling vintage objects to the first person who DMs to claim them has created a massive surge of interest in vintage in general, which means that not only are there a lot more amateur dealers out there competing with shoppers for great finds, but snagging those finds once they show up on Instagram has also become more competitive. It can be disappointing to miss out—especially when the algorithm shows you a post three days late—but it also re-creates some of the fun of vintage shopping IRL, because you have to get there first to get the best stuff. "That's part of the hype," explains Pip Newell, a Melbourne-based dealer who started one of the first Instagram vintage stores, Curated Spaces, in 2015. "People love that there's just one, and things sell so quickly. Stores comment 'SOLD' and their followers go crazy."

With all that pressure to be the first to buy, it's important to remember that overall, acquiring objects for your home should be a slow process that feels highly personal and considered. Because vintage does so much of the heavy lifting in the personality department, that goes double. When you first move into a new home, there are certain staples you'll probably need right away, like a bed or sofa or a bookshelf. On the rest, you can and should take your time, so you can buy things that are meaningful to you rather than just rushing to fill a space. "It ends up so much more interesting and so much more about you when you don't rush," says Wearstler. "You have time. You can travel, you can educate yourself. And you end up with things that make you really happy, which is what it's all about."

As you start shopping in earnest, here are a few key definitions and distinctions to keep in mind.

Quasimodo Chair by Daniel Weil and Gerard Taylor for Anthologie Quartett, 1988, courtesy of Éclectico Studio

"Antique" versus "vintage" versus "modern"

You might see these three terms used interchangeably to describe the era in which certain objects were made. However, they all mean something slightly different. Antiques are older and often more valuable; they're usually defined as being at least one hundred years old (think Chippendale chairs, Queen Anne consoles, or Louis XIV cabinets), though the term can be used a little more loosely sometimes. Vintage items are meant to be more than twenty years old, but less than a hundred, and ideally are somewhat reflective of the era in which they were created. Modern is a bit trickier. It can be used to mean contemporary or new, when it's used to talk about the general aesthetic of an object, but when it's used in the context of vintage shopping, it means an item made during the rise of the Modernism movement, in the early- to mid-twentieth century (as in the term "Mid-Century Modern"). Having a basic understanding of what these terms mean will make you a savvier shopper—and spare you a lot of confusion!

Anonymous versus attributed

Many people associate vintage shopping with searching for items made by big-name designers, like Charles and Ray Eames or Arne Jacobsen. But while it's nice to own one of those attributed objects, because you can trace their origins and (often) trust their quality, anonymous objects with no discernable creator attached have their own appeal. With anonymous things, it's not about the pedigree but about the aesthetic expression—and they can be just as beautiful and worthy of a spot in your home. "My husband and I have a painting that looks like a Miró, and was made in the same period. It's not any less cool of an object for us," says Gilbert. Emi Moore, owner of the cult online design store Casa Shop, agrees: "Just because it's not a designer piece doesn't mean it's not special. If it's handmade, it might still be one-of-a-kind. And we might be drawn to it because it has an interesting glaze, or the glassblower used an unusual cane." For Casa Shop, Moore specifically looks for works signed not by well-known designers but by obscure craftspeople, because you can still imagine or even research the person who made it, but it's more rare, so the odds are lower that someone else will end up with the same piece.

Originals versus reeditions

As noted earlier, an original vintage piece is one that was made at least twenty years ago. A reedition, or reproduction, is one where a brand took the original, old design of something and manufactured a contemporary version. So, for example, if Gino Sarfatti designed a lamp for Flos in the 1950s, and you purchased one made in the 1950s—or even in the 1970s—you'd call that an original. If you purchased the exact same lamp that Flos reissued and manufactured in 2018, that would be a reedition. Usually brands reissue old designs when the originals are in high demand but aren't easy to come by, so the reeditioned version often costs less than the original. Sometimes reeditions are made with newer, better technology, too. But even when an item has been reissued and can be purchased easily by anyone at, say, Design Within Reach, purists often still want the vintage version. "You want the iconic thing," says Fabiana Faria, who cofounded Coming Soon with Barquet. "You don't want the new one, you want the beat up one, the one that has character. Once it's been reeditioned, there's the potential of everyone having it, and the uniqueness of it fades." Gilbert, however, sees the upside: "There's no shame in buying a licensed reproduction. If you don't need it to be an investment, and you just need it to work for you, it's a design that's been tried and tested," she says.

For those who are committed to bringing home a true vintage piece, here's a quick roll call of where you might find them:

- Garage sales
- Estate sales
- Thrift stores
- Flea markets
- Antique malls
- Auctions
- Websites and apps (including eBay, Etsy, LiveAuctioneers, Everything But the House, 1stDibs, Facebook Marketplace, Craigslist, Nextdoor, Chairish)
- Vintage stores
- Galleries or dealers
- Family members' homes

We decided to ask the experts to share their best insider advice for shopping some of the sources in that list, but we also wanted to add two tips of our own. First, search alerts are a key feature offered by nearly every online marketplace for vintage objects—including eBay, Craigslist, and LiveAuctioneers—that interior designers swear by but few amateur shoppers know about. Once you learn about an object you'd like to own, whether it be general, like Art Deco lamps, or specific, like a Gio Ponti Superleggera chair, you can instruct these websites to email you each time a new item matches your search terms. So not only do you never miss out on what you want, but you may also become more educated in the process about what's out there in the category you're following and how much it typically sells for.

Second, when shopping in real life, looking for the weirdest object on the table can be a good initial approach—something you haven't seen before or something that visibly stands out from the other items around it. When we go to flea markets, for example, we've trained ourselves to scan for the most unusual or striking shapes and colors, then we move in for closer inspection. The thinking is that whatever catches our eye in that moment is probably what will catch someone else's eye in our living room, a great goal that makes for a useful starting point.

Now we'll turn it over to the experts to offer more tips on where to go, what to look for, and how to negotiate when you're shopping for vintage.

Swedish candelabra, circa 1900, courtesy of Ponce Berga & 1stDibs

Entremanos Chair by Andrés Nagel, 1988, courtesy of Éclectico Studio

above left: Teapot by John Prip,
circa 1975

left: Yellow Flash sculpture by Gerald
Laing, 1968

opposite: Vase by Angelo Barovier for
Barovier & Toso, 1952

All courtesy of Rago/Wright

SHOPPING GUIDES

Patrick Parrish

Parrish is a longtime antique dealer and founder of the eponymous New York design gallery.

FLEA MARKETS

● For the best finds, go very early, when dealers are setting up—at least an hour before sunrise. If the flea opens to the public at 7:00 a.m., show up at 5:30 a.m., even if you have to pay extra; 90 percent of all deals are done by the time the public gets in.

● If you see something you like, always say something positive. Dogging the merchandise will not get you a better deal.

● When negotiating, don't say "I'll give you $100." Instead say, "What would your best price be?" If they say $125, counter with, "Would you do $100 cash?" (Always have cash.) If you're polite and complimentary of the piece, the dealer will often say yes.

● If you spot a steal, don't draw attention to yourself. Just pick it up calmly before someone else does, pay the agreed-on price, and get out of the booth ASAP.

● Some of my best scores have come from "terrible" vendors—the junky, gritty types. "Good" dealers with a unified, sophisticated look may be easier to search, but the price will be much higher.

● Always bring the following to a flea market: a flashlight (if you don't need one, you're there too late), comfortable shoes, sunscreen, a hat, water, a big bag, and plenty of cash.

Carmen Nash

Nash is the Florida-based furniture dealer behind the
Instagram shop Loft and Thought.

● Move around the store swiftly, scanning for anything
that stands out visually. There's no specific way to tell where
the best items are hiding; you just need to find a method to
thoroughly cover a large space. Scanning is also a great way to
train your eye—subsequent visits will go even faster, because
you'll know what's where.

● Since you're shopping in person, you have the advantage
of being able to touch things, and you should. Shift tables
and chairs to check for sturdiness and craftsmanship. Inspect
things like pottery and ceramics for chips and cracks. Patina is
good, but there's a thin line where things cross into the "needs
repair" category.

● Antique malls that are super organized, polished, and
color-coded tend to know their product, which usually means
higher prices. Crowded, dusty, jam-packed places are always
a more desirable picking ground for pros because you're more
likely to find a great deal.

● If you find multiple great pieces, start a pile. Store owners
are usually great about holding things for you in a no-shop
zone. Stay hands-free so you can move freely around the store
and touch and examine other objects.

● Know your antique mall vendors. Make a mental note
of any booth where you find several things you love, so you
can visit it frequently. Meeting the vendor and forging a
relationship is always good, too, so you can ask to be kept in
the loop when they find new stuff.

● Visit the same antique mall multiple times if you can, and
get to know its turnover rate for new products so you know
how frequently to go. This is essential information for the
savvy antique-mall shopper.

John & Linda Meyers

Linda and John Meyers run Wary Meyers, a Maine-based soap and candle company, but are also known for documenting their garage-sale finds on Instagram.

● To find garage sales and estate sales near you, check estatesales.org, Craigslist, local newspapers, community bulletin boards, and garage sale apps like Yard Sale Treasure Map. Figure out the best route based on the various start times, beginning with the best sale first. Go to wealthier neighborhoods first. Odds are you'll find a higher quality of stuff.

● If something intriguing was mentioned in the ad but you don't see it at the sale, ask about it. The sellers may not have put it out yet. This happened to us once—we went to a sale for old airline posters, didn't see them, and assumed they sold. Then somebody asked about them and got to buy all the good ones for $5 each. It still stings, but we learned our lesson.

● Don't arrive at garage sales too early. This is called being an early bird, and it's not very courteous to the person trying to set up their sale. A maximum of thirty minutes may be fine, if you're nice about it. For especially promising estate sales, though, you may want to arrive early and wait in line.

● If there's something you *really* want but it doesn't have a price, don't ask about that first. Grab something else and ask about it, then put it down, making it seem like the price is too high or you can't afford it. Then ask about the item you really want, and the price might be better, if the host starts to feel like they may have overpriced things.

● Bring a variety of money with you: change, singles, fives. Nobody wants to change a twenty for a two-dollar item. And it's easier to get a six-dollar item for five if you're showing a five and not a ten!

● At estate sales, never forget to look in garages and basements.

Helena Barquet &
Fabiana Faria

Barquet and Faria founded Coming Soon, a New York boutique that offers colorful contemporary objects as well as vintage furniture.

AUCTIONS

● Beware of the buyer's premium, which is a fee that's added to anything you purchase after you win it. It can be as much as 25 percent above the selling price. Check the amount before you attend the auction.

● Auctions move very quickly, and you don't want to feel pressured to make decisions during the bidding process, so it's important to come prepared. Have your top bid amounts established before the sale starts, and stick to them.

● Get to an auction as early as possible to preview the lots and get a really good look at any items you're interested in, to assess their quality. Open all doors and drawers, look at the back, look underneath.

● Some larger furniture auctions let you use stickers to claim your pieces. The auctions open their doors, and the first interested party to put their sticker on a piece gets it. Stock up on dot stickers just in case.

● Try not to get too emotionally invested in any one piece. That's when you start making mistakes, like overbidding. Try to just enjoy the adventure of it—even if you lose that treasure.

● Always be aware of how you'll get a piece home. Most auctions will expect you to take it that day. Sometimes big, heavy pieces go for low amounts because moving them is so expensive.

Pip Newell

Newell is the dealer behind the most influential Instagram vintage store in Australia, Curated Spaces.

ONLINE

● First, find out which online marketplaces you have in your area, including possibly Craigslist, eBay, Gumtree, Facebook Marketplace, Everything But the House, LiveAuctioneers, or local online auction houses. You'll want to search all of these, because some days you'll have success on one but not the others.

● Look for potential, not perfection. Some of my best finds didn't look like much at first glance. I like to visually undress the photo, looking past the poor quality, the bad lighting, and the dingy interiors to see the item for what it is. Over time, you'll train your eye to do this automatically.

● Don't be tempted to only look in the area near your home. Open your search as far as the system allows—even to neighboring states. The perfect pieces are often worth having shipped. You can try uShip to get competitive rates (or look for a man-with-a-van on Craigslist or your local classifieds site), but always ask for written confirmation that the shipment will be insured, and ask the seller to photograph the item before it's picked up, in case it gets damaged in transit.

● Use very general search terms. You never know how someone will list their item if they don't know what it is or what material it's made of. One of my favorite sofas was listed as "Pink Thingy," whereas if someone has listed their piece as "Mid-Century Marble Coffee Table," they already know its value, and you won't get a bargain.

● Stay on top of your communication. Online marketplaces can be fast paced, and the good pieces don't last long, so be assertive and prompt with your replies. If you find something you like, try to lock in the sale right away.

● Don't be afraid to ask questions. If you want more or better photos, ask for them. If you're shipping the piece and can't inspect it yourself, ask the seller to make a specific list of any damage or flaws the piece may have.

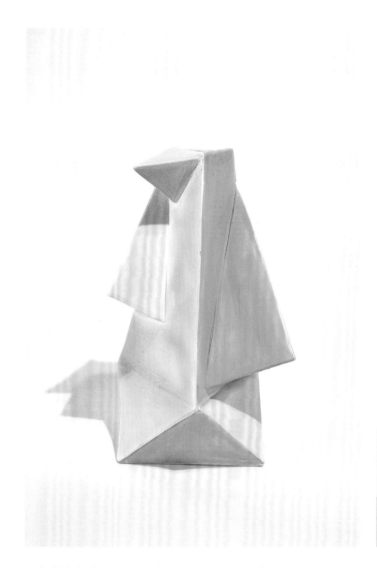

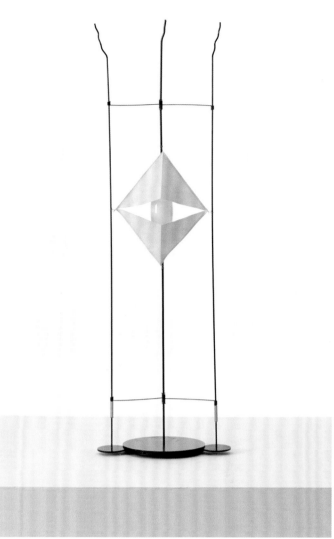

opposite: Sing Sing chair by Shiro
Kuramata, 1985, courtesy of Béton Brut

above left: Geometric ceramic vase,
date unknown, courtesy of Casa Shop

above right: Cheerioh Lamp by Bernhard
Dessecker and Susanne Maus for Ingo
Maurer, 1988, courtesy of Béton Brut

left: Compotier trèfle by Pablo Picasso,
1959, courtesy of Rago/Wright

BUYING

Finding a vintage object you're drawn to is a simple combination of luck + knowledge + gut instinct: You're walking a flea market, you happen to spot a Richard Sapper Tizio lamp, or an anonymous vase with an unusual shape you like, and you pick it up. But the question of what to do next—buy it or move on—is more complicated, because it's always a negotiation between an impulsive decision and an informed one. To explain, the number one cardinal rule of buying vintage, which you'll hear all the professionals repeat ad nauseum, is that he who hesitates is lost; if you put a piece down or try to sleep on it, the odds are it won't be there when you get back. Generally speaking, if you love it and can easily afford it, you should go for it, especially if it's not a particularly well-known piece. Yet if you aren't quite sure what you're looking at, or whether the asking price is fair, you may need to do a bit of research before you feel confident pulling the trigger. Ultimately the right balance between the two is going to be your call, especially if the risk in one direction (losing the item versus paying too much) feels significantly greater for you than in the other.

If you do decide to research before you buy, the best starting point is the fastest, most accessible one: Usually the dealer or seller will have at least some information about the piece, especially if it has any sort of attribution, so put their knowledge to use by asking questions. Useful ones might include the following:

- Who designed or manufactured this?
- What era is it from?
- Is it part of any particular design movement?
- How rare is it?
- How was it made or what is it made from?
- Does it have any flaws?
- Where did you find it?
- Is there any story to how you acquired it that makes it more special?

Any bit of information you can glean from the seller will help inform your decision making—not just in terms of whether an object is valuable, but also in terms of whether it has a backstory that's intriguing to you, and whether its characteristics will help it fit in well with your interior and with the rest of your collection. But if whatever the dealer knows is not enough, or you just want to do your own due diligence, you should inspect the piece yourself. An easy way to determine what the piece is and what it might be worth is with an approach we like to call the Three Ms: materials, maker, and market research.

Hill House 1 chair by Charles Rennie Mackintosh, 1902, produced by Cassina I Maestri Collection since 1973

Materials

"Materials" means attempting to identify what an object is made of, and how it was made. This helps you determine two things: how well it's constructed (and thus how high quality and potentially valuable it is) and whether it is, in fact, an original or old object versus something made more recently. The first step might be to figure out if it was made by hand or by machine. Of course, plastic is always made by machine, but if you're looking at glass, wood, metal, or ceramic, a handmade piece would typically be more rare than one that was mass-produced by the thousands in a factory. Telltale signs of mass-production in glass or ceramic include seams down the middle, or, in wood, joints or grains that are too perfect and symmetrical. Dovetail joints are more likely to be handmade, and heavier wood with no grain on the edges is more likely to be solid rather than less-expensive veneer. A metal object made by hand would often be more organic or imperfect in shape, and made of a pourable or more pliable material like bronze, brass, or sterling silver. And precious metals are almost always stamped with an identifier, such as "18k" or "925."

Knowing whether something is old or new is a little bit harder. If the piece is made of a material like raffia or Bakelite that's no longer used very often, or if it features a texture that was highly specific to one era, like lava glaze on mid-century pottery, that's helpful. But sometimes the clues are a lot more subtle. "Look for honest wear," Parrish advises. If you see scuffs or oxidization where they wouldn't naturally appear through normal usage, "then it probably means someone's deceptively trying to make the object look older than it is," he says.

Maker

The maker of a piece can refer to the person who made it by hand, like Isamu Noguchi or Hans Wegner, or the person who designed it for production, like Florence Knoll or Tapio Wirkkala. It can also refer to the brand or manufacturer that produced it, like Dansk or Herman Miller. More abstractly, you could also consider the place in which the object was made as part of its origin story, like glass from Murano or mid-century pottery from California. These are the most basic building blocks for identifying and properly valuing any vintage item, and if you decide to get more serious about collecting, they are the most important pieces of information to get good at sleuthing out. In general, if you can

verify the craftsperson, designer, artist, or producer behind a piece, there's a better chance it's going to be more valuable, especially if it's rare.

Sometimes that's as easy as turning it over and looking for a label or signature. Other times, you may have to dig deeper. Start by asking yourself if the object's shape or detail reminds you of any person or aesthetic movement that you're already familiar with—if so, you can look up whatever you do know on a big vintage site like 1stDibs, Pamono, or eBay and start scrolling for clues. Those sites are so big that they can act as convenient, free databases for information. You can also try to generalize whatever is the most defining element of the object—like tubular wooden legs, or a blue zigzag pattern—and try searching for that, just in case your find happens to show up. For those searches, we usually use either 1stDibs or Google Image search. It's amazing how many times we've wondered what a vintage piece is and identified it just by looking up a few keywords, including the chunky pine chairs that Monica got for free from a woman in Berlin that turned out to be designed in the 1970s by the Swede Rainer Daumiller.

If you have a hunch who the maker of an object might be but aren't sure, you can look at a book on that maker to check if it's included, or see if there's a corresponding Instagram hashtag for the maker, in case someone's posted a piece like yours before. You can also post the object on social media yourself in case any of your followers might know what it is (or can tag someone who would).

Market Research

If you specifically want to gauge what price makes sense for an object, it's time for some market research, which just means snooping online to see how much other people are charging for the same or similar thing—even if it means pulling out your phone in the middle of a store. First determine your best, most specific search term based on what you know, whether it's "Dansk Kobenstyle 2-quart pot" or something more generic like "ribbed sterling silver box." Then search Google, eBay, Etsy, Worthpoint, and/or LiveAuctioneers to see if anyone's sold one before. But be careful to check the price the item has actually sold for in the past, not the price that sellers are listing currently. Just because someone is asking $250 for an '80s flatware set doesn't mean they're going to get it. And like we said before,

Postmodern welded steel chairs, 1990s, courtesy of That Galerie & 1stDibs

vintage is a supply and demand market—the "correct" price for something is always a reflection of what collectors who really want it are willing to pay. That's why a fair ask for a Ligne Roset Togo sofa may have been $1,500 ten years ago, but is five times that amount now that people are tripping over one another to own one.

There's one more major consideration to take into account before buying a vintage object, and that's what condition it's in. The TL;DR here is, don't be afraid to buy something that's a little imperfect—honest wear, like Parrish said, is usually inevitable with old things, and imperfections can add to a piece's character and make it easier to live with. "So many people are afraid to touch things that look shiny and new and glossy," says Barquet. "But something that's been around for so long, with nicks and scratches, you're more comfortable and at ease around it." Adds Newell, "When they see that patina, some people freak out, but I adore it. The wear is part of the object's story. It feels more homey, more lived-in."

Not to mention, you can always rehab the object. When we look at vintage items, we try to envision what their potential could be. Can we strip an extraneous layer of paint off a console and restore it to its original wood finish? Can we watch a YouTube video to reupholster the seat pads of those dining chairs in a better fabric? Sometimes that's the best way to own something fantastic at an affordable price. But not always—having a lounge chair or a sofa professionally reupholstered, for example, is wildly expensive, and if you pledge to do a restoration project yourself, make sure you're really going to follow through with it, otherwise it's not worth the initial purchase. You'll also need to be careful if the piece you're buying is well known and a significant investment, because with true collector's items, restoration can detract from value, so it's often better to live with them in their original state, however flawed.

Whether an object is imperfect or perfect, famous or anonymous, just remember that whatever you pay or whatever it is doesn't matter so much if you love it and want to live with it for a while. Sometimes the very best purchases are driven by pure, blinding emotion rather than common sense. "When we first opened Coming Soon, we bought a Pepsi machine," says Barquet. "We drove to Albany in a snowstorm to go get it, and we couldn't fit it into the trunk, so we had to drive back to New York through a blizzard with the trunk open. We didn't even like Pepsi, but we had to have it. How do you explain that? It's completely irrational."

Of course, as noted above, you should be careful not to get too emotional over a piece in case the sale doesn't work out, which happens a lot in the vintage game. Parrish told us a great story about his biggest-ever fail, which happened a few years back at a flea market. "I saw this $700 sculpture of a snail, with peeling white paint, and I didn't buy it," he recalls. "The third time I came around to look at it, it was gone. Later I overheard a friend talking about the Giacometti bronze he'd found, in the shape of a snail, and I felt sick. Then it was worth $200,000; now, it's about a million. But I didn't let it bum me out—I use experiences like that to fuel myself, to know that stuff is out there and I have to keep looking. If you let your mistakes inspire you, you can continue to find great things."

When you get into buying vintage, it's inevitable that you'll make all kinds of mistakes, and that's 100 percent okay. We've all bought something thinking it was some cool obscure thing, and it turned out to be from Ikea. We've all paid too much for something, or changed our minds about it later. Acquiring and living with vintage objects is a messy, imprecise process, and value is fairly unpredictable, so it's better to accept the occasional failure as part of the price of success. It's worth it for that incredible, profound feeling of scoring something you love; plus, if you do end up hating it later, you can always resell it. It had a life before you, and it can have a new one after you, too.

above: Flatware/salad servers, year unknown, from the collection of Kelsey Heinze

right: Les Trois Suisses table by Philippe Starck, 1982, courtesy of Rago/Wright

opposite: Parola lamp, model 268, by Gae Aulenti & Piero Castiglioni for Fontana Arte, 1980, courtesy of Rago/Wright

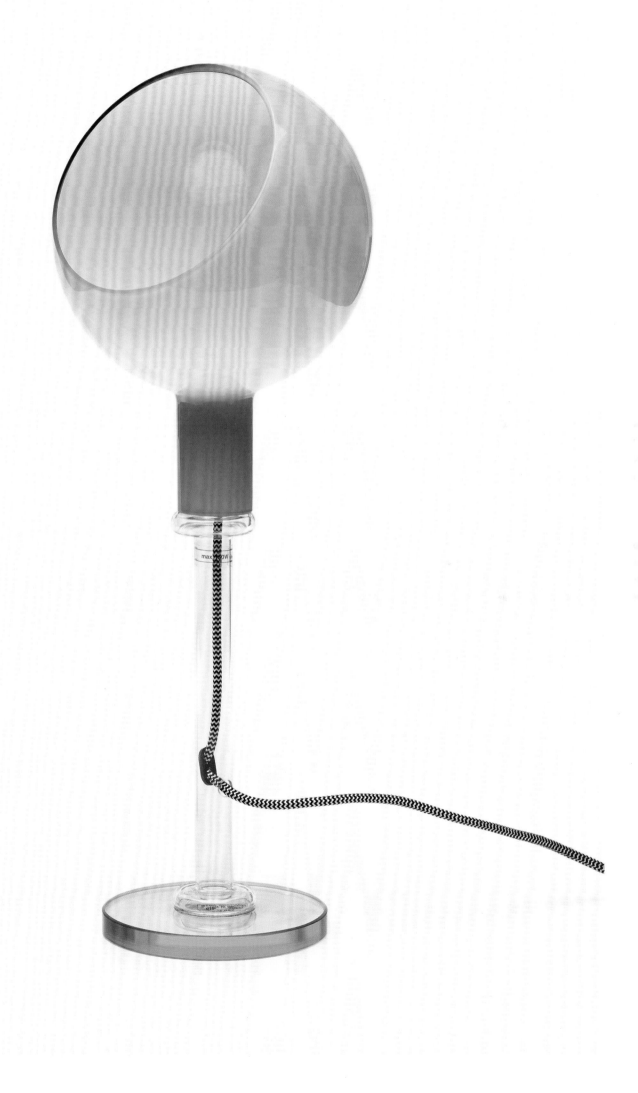

HÉLÈNE REBELO & EDOUARD BEAUGET

Rebelo and **Beauget** are cofounders of the online shop Cool Machine, which is dedicated to contemporary handmade objects. Rebelo is also an interior design consultant and curator, work she's landed partly thanks to her popular personal Instagram, where she shares hyper-colorful design and fashion inspiration. Her style—and her insatiable vintage-hunting habit—is reflected in the airy loft she and Beauget share in Brussels.

" I'm a lifelong bargain-hunter. The secondhand furniture and decor I find, I use in my work or my private life, or resell in Brussels. When we decorate, though, we always favor secondhand because Edouard, like me, has been going to flea markets from an early age."

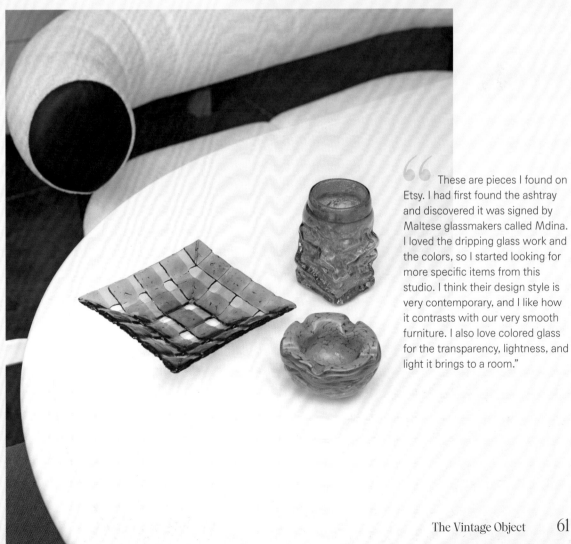

" These are pieces I found on Etsy. I had first found the ashtray and discovered it was signed by Maltese glassmakers called Mdina. I loved the dripping glass work and the colors, so I started looking for more specific items from this studio. I think their design style is very contemporary, and I like how it contrasts with our very smooth furniture. I also love colored glass for the transparency, lightness, and light it brings to a room."

"Our loft is part of an industrial complex that used to be a lamp factory. We've always lived in small flats, so when we came here, we had to adjust to bigger rooms. We needed a big dining table so it wouldn't look ridiculous. I found this oval wooden table thirty minutes from Brussels, in a classified ad from a man who was getting rid of his company's furniture; this conference table had been sleeping in his garage for months. It was eighty euros, and the perfect dimensions for our loft, but the top was coated in thick, black plastic and the legs were a very orange wood. I decided to repaint it. My inspiration at the time was Gustaf Westman's tables, or Love House's in New York: oval, monochrome tables with remarkable legs. My dad's a great handyman who was always customizing our furniture at home, and he taught me how to transform things according to my taste. In the end, we got the perfect table for less than two hundred euros, and since this shoot, it's found its final color: a warm, raspberry red."

"I pay a lot of attention to the amount of money I invest. Sometimes I wait months to find a piece at a reasonable price. I have a lot of love for design, but when it comes to secondhand, I think patience is the key word. If you're patient, you can always find great deals."

"We already had the green Orsay chairs by Gae Aulenti in our old flat, which we brought in from France. We love the bright-green vintage-wool fabric with the white lacquered metal frames. The frames contrast with the material and highlight the rounded seats. My choices are often either very geometric, or very rounded and smooth."

"Living in a larger, more open apartment is a challenge, because you have to mix colors, shapes, and materials in a single space. I learn day by day to create harmony."

"I really like to play with shapes in the furniture, so in our house you'll find a lot of spheres, squares, and cylinders. For example, the Steiner coffee table from the '70s is square with rounded corners, and our white shelf and Herman Miller Chiclet sofa have the same shape." ←

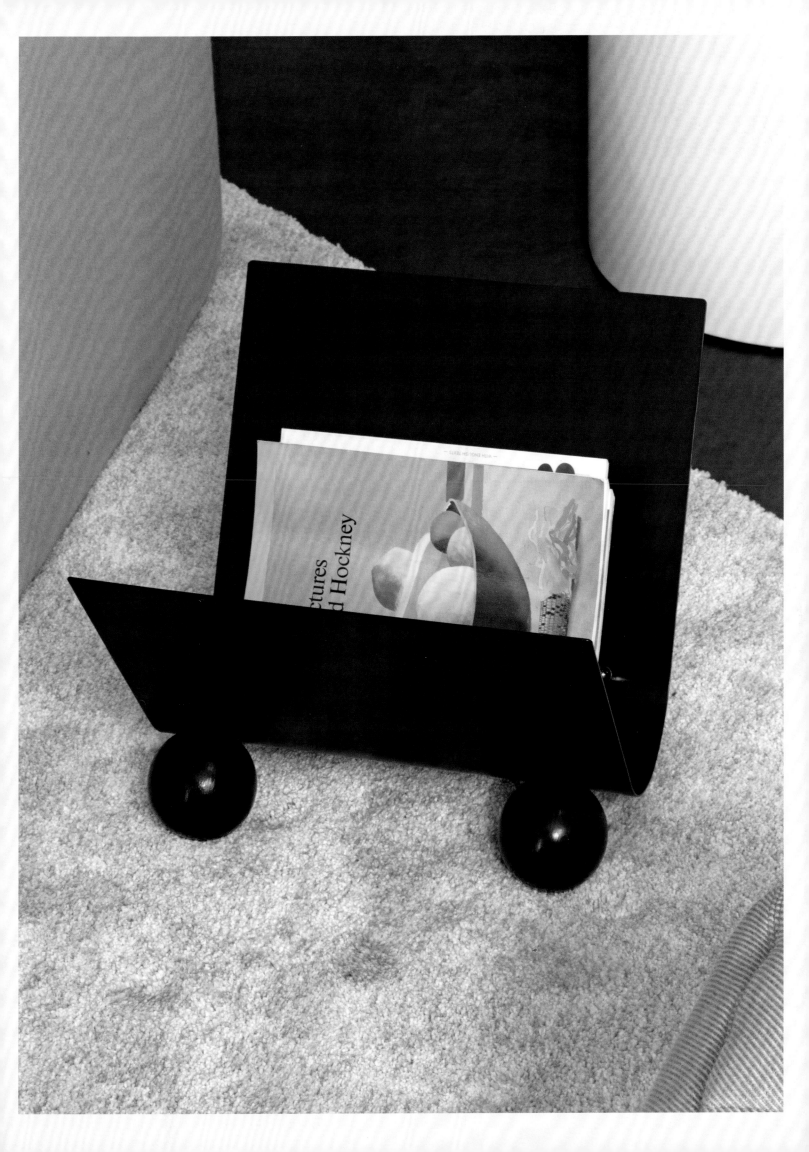

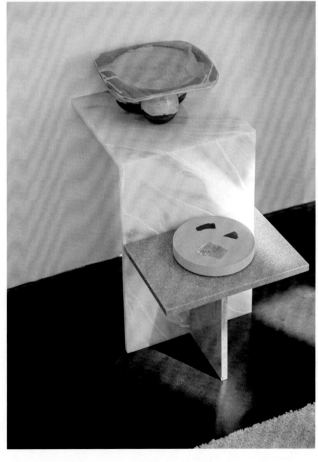

 Our flat has seen many pieces of furniture and objects come and go over time; nothing is really fixed here. Our decoration changes according to our finds. I love objects, but I'm not materialistic, and I have no problem parting with a piece."

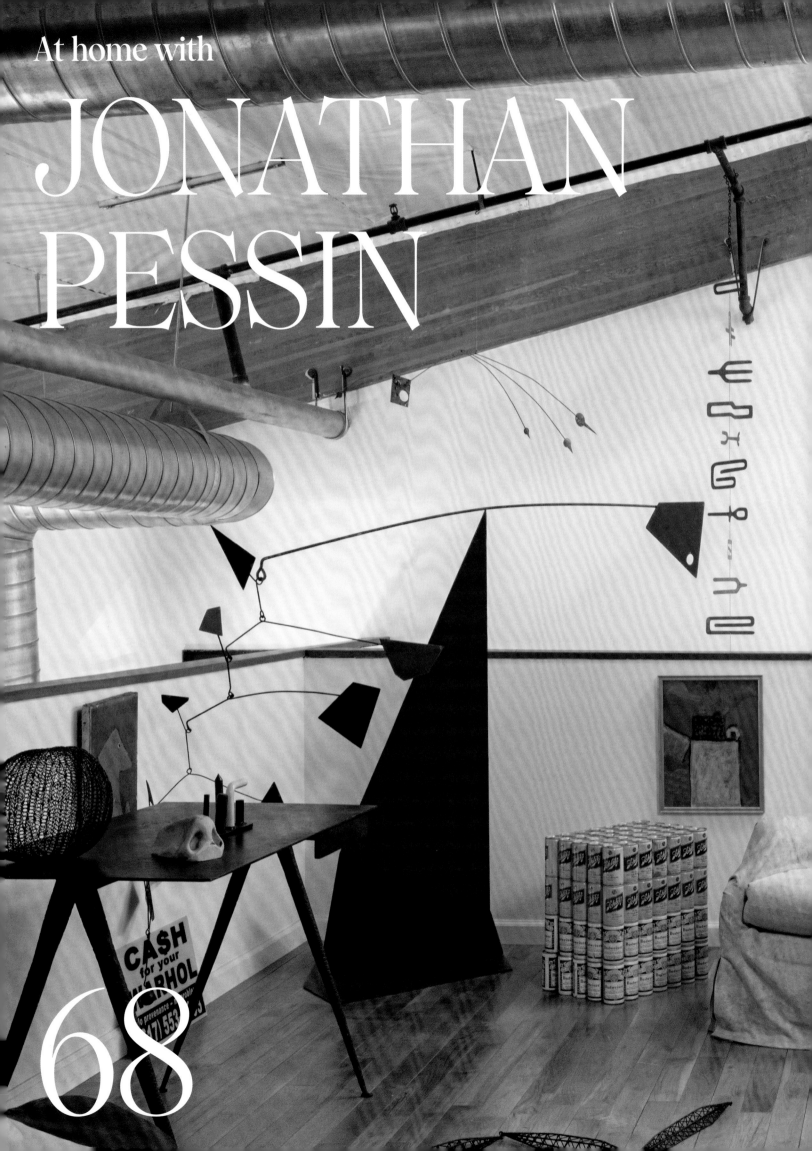

At home with

JONATHAN PESSIN

68

"I like having something that was never meant or intended to be used as a domestic object. For instance, that papier-mâché hand chair. It's so amateur. Is it a foot? Is it a hand? I like things out of context, and a giant hand is so out of context."

A collector with a penchant for the oversized and the absurd, **Pessin** runs the cheekily named vintage showroom Not For Sale from a giant space next to his loft in Los Angeles. The boundary between the two spaces is practically nonexistent, as he cycles in favorite finds like a giant Mr. Goodbar, a papier-mâché Bart Simpson, and, always, French industrial furniture from the 1950s.

" I love French industrial design—anything Prouvé-esque, or Charlotte Perriand-esque. Because those pieces are so expensive, I actually like finding someone's anonymous inspired version of something. Under my desk are these perforated shelves that I bought at a flea market. They seemed French industrial and super cool; anything metal and perforated is a magic combination for me. People have tried to buy them, and I'll always be like, 'They're not for sale.' Somebody saw them in a picture I posted, and they asked, 'Do you know what those are? They're from a supermarket freezer, to put produce in.' For a second, I was kind of bummed, but now anytime someone comes to my loft and wants them, I won't sell them, but I will say, 'By the way, do you know what they are?' Because it's a great story." ←

"Part of the reason I named the store Not For Sale is that one of my superpowers is I can go into any store, and the first thing I pick, they're like, 'Welllll, that's the one thing not for sale.' It annoys me because I'm like, 'You're a store. You shouldn't have it in there if it's not for sale!' The way I justify it for myself is, well, it's my brand, it's in the name—so you can't get mad at me."

"I don't like practical things, so if I have to have a practical object, I want a giant version of it that renders it impractical, like a giant toothbrush. I like absurdity and anything oversized. I like having a playful element. I missed out on this giant rotary phone recently. It was three feet long, and in my head, it would have been the perfect thing to have where most people would have a coffee table. Of course, now I'm trying not to buy oversized things because I don't want to be known as the guy who collects all the oversized things." →

" The Peter Shire Olympic torch is a special piece. I had seen them before, but most of the ones out there are shorter, like 10 feet. I think this one is 14 feet, and it's actually the one that was in the 1984 Olympic Village. I went to a friends' sale, and this was in pieces on the floor. I knew just from seeing the curved stem what it was. After I bought it, somebody wanted to buy it from me, and at first, I was going to sell. But then I was like, 'I don't want to sell this thing. It's too weird and cool; what a perfect piece for this space.' It's not exactly my vibe. I like Postmodern, but it's a little whimsical for me. But the scale of it is so good. And the honest answer is that the more people like something in my loft, the less inclined I am to let it go." ←

"The life-size papier-mâché Mies van der Rohe has a good story. The California mid-century architect Craig Ellwood was teaching a class in the '50s or '60s and had Mies come talk to his students. The students made this for Mies as a gift, and then it stayed in Ellwood's office until it went to LA Modern Auctions, where it lived in their warehouse for ten years. I don't think it was important enough for them to auction. They had a big warehouse sale, and when I walked in, it was all mostly mid-century furniture, which is not my thing. I walked past this thing—it was in a nook, and it had a price tag of $75— and I was like, done."

"There's this desire for me to have the thing that no one else has. I can love something, and then as soon as I find out someone else has one, I'm kind of over it. I spend so much time and energy thinking about objects, probably in an unhealthy way. An old therapist would say I'm narcissistically attached to them, but it's part of my brand. It's NFS, not for sale. I want to keep everything, but a lot of the things that I *think* I want, when I get them, I don't anymore. I love the hunt. I like the story of finding it and how things come to me."

78

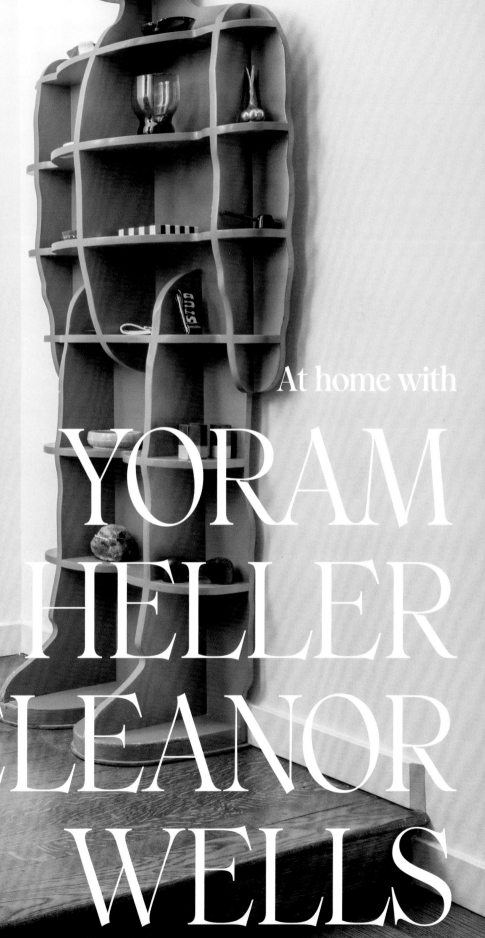

At home with

YORAM HELLER & ELEANOR WELLS

Before they met, **Heller and Wells** were both obsessive collectors—Heller of both furniture and businesses (he's an investor in Yola Mezcal, the cannabis brand Sunday Goods, and the coffee chain Go Get Em Tiger, among others) and Wells of vintage clothing, a massive archive of which she rents out when she's not working as a party promoter. The pair now live together in a maximalist Los Angeles Craftsman designed in collaboration with Charlap Hyman & Herrero.

" *[previous spread]* We got both the John Risley Lady Chairs and the Ueli and Susi Berger bookshelf at auction. When we moved in together, it emerged that we both had a penchant for human figural furniture. A lot of faces, a lot of people. The whimsy of it, maybe. The bookshelf typically houses Eleanor's collection of twenty or thirty antique hair combs. Her mother was big into antiques and always said everyone has to collect something, so she arbitrarily chose combs. Unfortunately, an earthquake or two has brought a few of them tumbling down. There are also a lot of salt and pepper shakers, and ceramic matches by the artist Seth Bogart, whose work has a gay–meets–*Pee-wee's Playhouse* vibe." ←

" The chairs are by Ettore Sottsass. Yoram's brother gifted him a piece of stained glass for his birthday, and when he met the artist, David Scheid, he said, 'What if we do the whole door in stained glass?' They worked collaboratively and came up with the design and colors. Yoram and his brother have this thing where they try to outdo each other with the most ridiculous, expensive birthday gifts possible. Most recently, because Yoram picked up a tennis racket, the next thing you know we get a ball machine sent to us. The feet are the base of a dog bowl made by the ceramics studio Male Glaze. The wallpaper is Fornasetti. The rug is by Charlap Hyman & Herrero for Schumacher." →

"The painting in our hallway is by a guy named Richard Lindner. Yoram's dad was a chemist at Caltech, and in his mid seventies he started collecting a bunch of art as a hobby—he just buys art all day, scouring all these weird auctions. He got this crazy piece and decided to give it to us. The vase was an Etsy find, by a French artist named Rémi Lacombe. The bench is made from Marmoreal—the terrazzo tile designed by Max Lamb for Dzek—left over from our bathroom, which is entirely lined in it. We have all sorts of random bits and bobs made from it—the bench, a little table, a few trash cans, funny pieces. You can do anything with it, and it's so much cheaper to make this bench from leftover slabs than buying a new marble bench. If you're slightly resourceful, finding someone to make something like this is relatively easy to do." ←

"The pink ashtray on the bar cart is by Sottsass, and the vase is an Eleanor find. She loves trompe l'oeil. It has a swept-up-piece-of-fabric look that reminds her of *Beauty and the Beast*. The sofas are Ubald Klug. When Yoram bought them, one sofa was fine and one was in worse condition, then our dog Georgio went to town on them and neither one is in great condition anymore. We love our dog, though—we have to keep reminding ourselves that. The Nicola L lamp we got at auction. Jim Walrod used to be married to a friend of Yoram's, and he taught Yoram a lot about furniture. Jim had an orange Nicola L commode in his house that Yoram really loved. Very shortly after Nicola died, this lamp came up at auction, and Yoram got it, but he got lucky—it was at the beginning of a bidding war for these pieces, and now they're astronomical." →

"Yoram's brother sent him a link to this tuxedo cabinet right at the beginning of quarantine, from an auction house in Italy. He sends us the wildest things. We were lying in bed and Yoram was like, 'Should I bid on it?' Then we woke up and he was like, 'I won!' The details are insane. The arms articulate out, and the pockets on the front open. Even the buttons have little pieces of leather on them. Usually we keep a face vase on it, or a '70s scuba diver ice bucket, so it looks like it has a head. The plates are all Heller, which is Yoram's last name, so we have a huge set." ←

"The glasses in this bedroom were Eleanor's first contribution to the house. She found them on Etsy, and they were from a 1960s French optician's shop. They light up from behind. The curtains are by Josef Franck, and we love them because they were made in the 1920s, but they're so trippy. There really was something so anachronistic about the 1920s. The fiberglass bed was designed by a guy named Mark Held for the French brand Prisunic, in the 1960s, and on it is an E blanket, for Eleanor, but made by Everybody.World. The founders were Yoram's first and only bosses, when he was an intern at American Apparel in the early 2000s." ←

COLLECTORS' ITEMS

There are different levels of commitment to "the hunt," depending on the magnitude of your desire and the number of hours available in your day. First there are the dabblers—those who have saved searches on all of the online platforms, and who make it a point, when they land in a new town, to hit the best thrift stores and flea markets. Then there are more serious collectors, who arrive at an estate sale hours before it opens, who plan vacations around a Google map pinned with antique stores and fairs, and who commandeer shipping crates full of goodies scored from auction houses across the Atlantic. The third level consists of the truly—and some might say pathologically—vintage-obsessed, whose means of acquiring something they covet can range from months of stalking to outright subterfuge. These are our people, and we're featuring five of their most prized finds in the following pages.

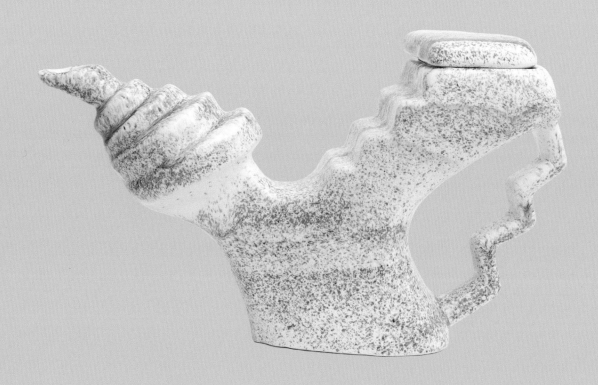

Abigail Campbell
vintage dealer, Abigail Bell Vintage, Miami

" I found this teapot while doing an eBay search for weird pottery one night, as you do. It wasn't marked very well, so no one would have found it. It didn't have any identification besides a mysterious 'N' signature on the bottom, but I loved it, and the bidding was at $5, so I got it for maybe $12 with shipping. It arrived, I was obsessed with it, and it kickstarted an idea of collecting teapots, but weird sculptural or artist-made ones. That's now grown into a collection of sculptural pitchers, strange vases, and studio pottery in general.

Sometimes when I find something I get this feeling that it was meant for me—that maybe that's why it was buried on eBay and had the wrong keywords. It's like it was waiting for me, knowing that's the only way I'd be able to afford it. And with this teapot, it felt like I was the only one who could appreciate it, too. I showed it to so many people and they were like, 'Oh, okay, cool.' My mom asked, 'Did someone in high-school art class make that?' For me, a child could have made it, it doesn't matter; it's about how it makes you feel. I've always been fascinated with pieces by no-name people, or art students, where maybe that's the only thing they've ever made. The pieces that don't get any recognition.

That said, I've since discovered that this teapot is by the Florida studio potter Charles Nalle. It's wild. Is it even supposed to be functional? And why did everyone make weird teapots in the '80s? I don't even like tea, which is the funniest part."

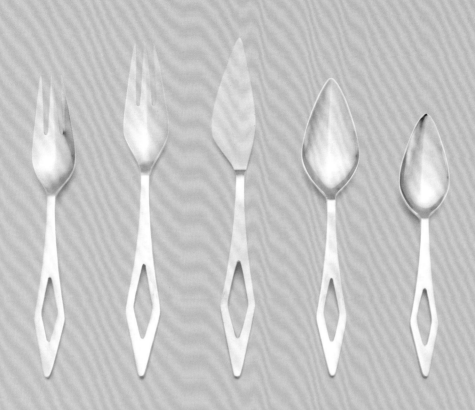

Dung Ngo

editor, *August Journal*, New York City

"Collecting has always been a part of my life—although a better word would be 'accumulating.' I've had three significant collections. The first was right after college, when I was obsessed with plywood. After a few years, my living room looked like a Mid-Century Anonymous meeting, with a dozen or so mismatched plywood chairs. In order to exorcise the bug, I wrote a book about the history of plywood furniture, *Bent Ply*, then was able to promptly de-accession the collection. The next fever was with Olivetti typewriters, and I accumulated designs by Mario Bellini, Ettore Sottsass, Marcello Nizzoli, and more before donating them all to SFMOMA. After that, I wanted to find something I could collect that fulfilled a few criteria: a typology that's not on collectors' radars, and therefore would be relatively affordable, and something small enough to let me keep the entire collection in a closet without renting out storage space. Flatware filled the niche.

Postwar Italians believed that architects should be able to design everything, 'from the spoon to the city,' and a big part of my collection is flatware by architects. I often look for flatware by the polymath Gio Ponti, even going so far as to sneak a few teaspoons from his collection at the Parco dei Principi Hotel in Sorrento, Italy, at breakfasts during my stay there. Ponti's Domus flatware in particular embodies his signature diamond pattern (which he applied to everything from spoons to buildings). Named after the magazine he founded, Domus was more form than function, and therefore wasn't in production for very long. I was lucky to find these pieces at a flea market many years ago, and they remain a prized cornerstone of my collection."

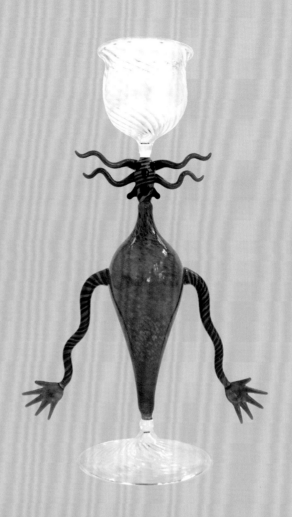

Sally Simms

vintage dealer, Super Saturday, Charleston

" I've always been into interiors, and I've always been a nester, ever since I was a kid. In college, I realized that you could get more beautiful stuff more affordably if you were interested in older things, so I started buying vintage objects locally. At first, I was selling out of practicality. I would buy something for my home, style it, enjoy it for a bit, and then sell it with the styled photo. Eventually it occurred to me that I could do more curation—and not be limited to what I was styling into my own house—if I just accepted that I was a dealer.

This is one of the first things that I explicitly bought thinking, 'I'm a dealer now.' It came in a collection of art glass from an estate in New Jersey, three glass cups that were each unique. One of them has a figural lady standing on a flower holding a cordial glass, another says 'wow' and has a spunky little arrow, and then there's this guy. He was immediately the mascot; he has so much more personality than the others. He's wibbly and weird. He doesn't exactly have normal facial features, but he's anthropomorphic. I haven't seen another one like it. Someone tried to buy it from me, but I sent her an invoice and she never paid. I was so relieved, and ended up keeping it for myself."

Stephen Markos
design gallerist, Superhouse, New York City

" I was a follower of the late legendary collector Jim Walrod since forever. Although I didn't know him personally, he was a huge inspiration, and what I found interesting about his point of view was that he had all of these exquisite and expensive pieces of design that he didn't seem to treat too preciously—lamps on his kitchen countertops, piled up in his bedroom, etc. I loved that idea.

I had seen his Shigeaki Asahara lamp on Instagram, and I would look for it from time to time. I *never* saw it available anywhere. When Jim died, and Wright did an auction of his personal collection in 2018, I didn't get a chance to bid on his lamp, which only fueled my hunt. I kept searching. One day, the Paris gallery A1043 posted a picture on Instagram of their space and, in the corner, part of the Shigeaki lamp was in view. I immediately DM'ed them, but the gallery owner, Didier, told me it was in his private collection and he didn't intend to sell it. After some back-and-forth, he did agree to sell it to me, but he told me I was lucky because later the same day, one of his collectors came into the gallery and wanted to buy the lamp. Since he had already promised it to me, I got it.

In the end, it's one of my most favorite things. It very subtly references Memphis while not being in-your-face about it. It also feels like I have a little connection to Jim here. I did ask Didier if he'd purchased it from Wright, but he said no, it was from an Italian collector."

Toby Ziff

vintage dealer, Two Poems, London

66 I had seen this wonderful, whimsical jug on eBay when I was just starting out with Two Poems. It stayed on my watch list for an eternity, as the seller had it listed as collection-only in Wales, which is miles away from me. It was only listed for £25, but the seller wouldn't mail it under any circumstances. I tried to offer him triple what it would cost him to send it, but he wasn't bothered. Finally, I decided to hire a man-with-a-van who could go and collect it for me, because I just had to have it. The seller's house was deep in the countryside, and despite a nightmare finding the house, Ant—the driver—managed to retrieve the jug and give the man the cash.

During this trip, Ant picked up a few other pieces of pottery for me nearby, to make the job worthwhile. But that evening, on his way back from the house, he was driving through a dark and narrow country road, and as he was going up a hill, he noticed a car coming right up to his bumper behind him. Another car suddenly came out to block the road ahead. Some mob had tactically organized it so he'd have nowhere to go. They got out of their cars and proceeded to try to rob the van. Little did they know, though, that Ant is an ex–police officer, six-foot-five, and built to bits. He grabbed the baseball bat he keeps under his seat, got out the van, hit one of them, and they both scrambled away. He got back in the van and swerved as he accelerated quickly to get away. During this, all of my pottery went flying, and sadly broke. However, one thing remained completely unharmed: the wonderful jug."

92

Ombré Glass Chair by Germans Ermičs, 2017

THE CONTEM-PORARY OBJECT

When you're shopping for things to buy for your home—or even just scrolling Instagram for inspiration—it's easy to understand what qualifies an object as vintage: Is it more than twenty years old? Defining an object as contemporary, however, is an altogether more ambiguous task. A logical rule of thumb would seem to follow, that a contemporary object is any object made within the last twenty years. But, as with most rules, there's a gray area, because while some objects can't be classified as contemporary by age alone, they still *feel* contemporary in spirit.

That's because the defining idea of contemporary design is that its objects reflect the present era in some meaningful way, whether through the use of current technology, an exploration of new materials, a reflection of a zeitgeist-y trend, an engagement with current social or cultural issues, or a novel reinvention of historical forms. This notion transcends specific years, scales, and price ranges, so that contemporary design can encompass everything from Soft Baroque's irregularly shaped wooden tables, whose forms were inspired by Photoshop painting tools, to James Shaw's pastel-colored toilet-paper holders, which he makes by using an extrusion gun to sculpt recycled plastic in midair. It can refer to George Sowden's Memphis-y color-blocked peppermills for Hay or Studio Anansi's burl-wood consoles for CB2. It can be the chair you commissioned from a designer across the world or the checkerboard ashtray you picked up at your neighborhood coffee shop.

It can also be objects that were conceived many decades ago but still feel relevant to the current conversation. David Alhadeff, founder of the design store and gallery The Future Perfect, dates the contemporary era all the way back to the early 1990s, when a collective of designers known as Droog emerged in the Netherlands. Whereas design before had largely been either functional or decorative (or both), Droog's work was conceptual, introducing us to things like a chair made from an open web of knotted rope, stiffened with resin; a chandelier made from frosted glass milk bottles; and a chest consisting of twenty different discarded dresser drawers, bound together by a luggage strap. Droog's work still feels contemporary because it embodied so many of the traits we now associate with design: It was funny, whimsical, concerned with its environmental impact, and curious as to the possibilities of emerging technologies.

Brent Dzekciorius—the London design advisor who founded the architectural surfaces brand Dzek, which manufactures Max Lamb's large-scale take on terrazzo—defines contemporary design even more broadly. "I think if you're alive and you're making, then you're contributing to the contemporary landscape," he says. "What makes contemporary design is living people being creative." Think of Gaetano Pesce, the legendary Italian designer who still churns out editions of his rubbery 1984 Pratt chair from a studio in the Brooklyn Navy Yard, or Peter Shire, a founding member of the 1980s-era Memphis Group, whose splatter-painted mugs—hand-rolled in his Los Angeles studio since the 1970s—adorn the shelves of pretty much every creative person you know. Even though these objects were originally designed decades ago, you wouldn't look at one made last week and think, "A-ha, that's vintage!" And if Pesce and Shire are still

making them, that's only because their relevance to the current moment has kept demand for them so strong.

Despite the ambiguity of certain individual objects, however, we like to chart what we refer to generally as "the contemporary design era" back to right around the time of the 2008 global financial crisis and, coincidentally, just before Sight Unseen was founded. This was a time when several important things were happening at once. One was that independent designers—who had previously made a living working for large firms, or licensing their designs to manufacturers—began realizing the potential of the globally connected Internet as a platform for reaching consumers directly, which enabled them to begin manufacturing and selling products entirely on their own. Freed from the constraints of working with clients, or relying on brands to produce and distribute their work, designers began experimenting in the studio with materials and techniques, in some cases even inventing their own—ultimately ushering in a whole new aesthetic for design. If mid-century modern was all about beautifying the fruits of mass production, when we look back on this time, we'll think of designers who were breaking the rules of production entirely: Swedish-Chilean designer Anton Alvarez, who invented a giant thread-wrapping machine that binds anything that passes through it with colorful resin-soaked string, or Detroit-based designer Chris Schanck, who hand-foils his carved-foam furniture with layers of the paper-thin metallic sheets normally used to wrap chocolate.

The end of the aughts also happens to be the time when people started asking questions about where the things they were buying came from, in large part because the design

opposite: Rong Collection (Rong Chair) by Mario Tsai Studio, 2019
above: Daisy sconce by Eny Lee Parker, 2021

process was becoming more personal and less anonymous, while manufacturing was becoming more global and opaque. This more considered way of looking at objects—which ensured that a person's consumption aligned with their principles—also coincided with the slow food movement. But in design, it was less about knowing which mill in Italy the lumber for your dining table came from and more about attaching a face and a name to it. It was about creating a narrative and a personal connection to your objects. Which is, of course, not only the primary lesson of this book but also the idea we've been proselytizing since founding Sight Unseen: that there's value in getting to know the story behind the objects you choose to live with.

A glimpse behind the curtain

So yes, technically speaking, whether an object counts as contemporary mostly comes down to when it was made (the answer being . . . recently-ish?). But a funny thing happens when you subject it to the other classic inquiries of who, what, where, why, and how: The more of those questions you can answer, the more interesting—and often the more collectible—that contemporary object tends to be. While a decorative vase purchased at a big-box store has the what (a vase) and the where (likely in Asia), a vase purchased from a ceramicist in San Francisco who posts her hand-coiling process on Instagram comes with a full 360-degree story, which elevates the piece and gives it character. That's why we've seen big brands like West Elm and CB2 focusing on local creative communities and bringing design personalities to the fore over the last decade or so.

It's also why the behind-the-scenes documentation of process that's so prevalent on social media and sites like Sight Unseen has helped elevate independent design from a niche practice into a thing that everyone cares about. In addition to being a kind of passive education about what's cool, on-trend, interesting, or simply for sale right now in design, it's just plain fun to catch a glimpse behind the curtain, whether you're peeking inside Chen Chen & Kai Williams's Brooklyn studio as they slice apart stones to use as tabletops or following along as Thai-American designer Robert Sukrachand visits the village outside Bangkok where he makes cast-brass bells. It makes the work less rarefied and more relatable, even for those who have zero design knowledge otherwise.

This is a major aspect of what separates collecting vintage objects from collecting contemporary ones: While it may never be possible to know the story behind every vintage piece you collect, you can be an active participant in creating a narrative for your contemporary items by educating yourself, getting to know makers, understanding the conditions that brought these things into the world, and generally bringing an awareness and intention to your stuff—regardless of your budget.

A kind of patronage

A huge part of the appeal of collecting contemporary objects lies in feeling like you're perhaps a small part of one of those behind-the-scenes stories. Buying contemporary design, no matter the price, amounts to a kind of patronage, and when you can actually visualize what the designer's studio looks like, the kind of equipment they use, or the trips they take for inspiration, it makes a purchase that much more meaningful. "When it comes to buying furniture, generally I like to give my money and support to people who are living their lives in a creative way," says Dzekciorius, whose London home is filled with work by nearby designers and friends like Peter Marigold, Max Lamb, and Bernadette Deddens and Tetsuo Mukai of Study O Portable. "Prouvé's dead, you know? But if you buy something from a living designer, I like the idea that you're keeping the cycle of creativity moving."

For other people, the appeal of buying a piece of contemporary design is the prospect that you might end up owning a (possibly valuable) piece of future history. "I often think in terms of historical relevance, and analyzing whether a piece adds to a certain design discourse or not," says Chamber Projects founder Juan Mosqueda, who mounts exhibitions of up-and-coming designers like Jumbo and Objects of Common Interest from his home base in Buenos Aires. "If something is repetitive or derivative of certain stylistic concerns from the past, or it has nothing new to bring to the table, then I would probably pass."

But how to assess an item's potential as a future heirloom? And what about the role that emotion plays in deciding if you're committed enough to a piece of design to make your relationship status permanent? We'll be covering those topics and more in this chapter, but it's important to note that while we'll be talking about how considerations like materials and the market might affect your decision, you should absolutely not discount your immediate gut reaction when buying a piece of contemporary design—or, really, any of the object genres in this book. First, says Friedman Benda's Alex Gilbert, "You kind of have to love a piece, and then you can dig a little further, to understand the designer's practice, or where they're coming from, or what interests them. That's the moment where you're like, okay, this isn't just lust—this is love."

above left: Chubby Vase by Wang & Söderström for Hay, 2020

above right: Support vessel by Aldo Bakker for Karakter, 2016

left: Kat Bench by Studio POA, 2021, courtesy of Love House

opposite: Guise Floor Lamp by Odd Matter for Nilufar Gallery, 2019

INSPIRATION

At Sight Unseen, we've spent years shining a light into the far-off reaches of contemporary design, unearthing new talents, going into studios to find out how objects are made, and featuring the galleries and stores that sell those objects. But even with easily available resources like our site, if you haven't spent years curating your own aesthetic and cultivating a wish list of designers, it isn't easy to know where to begin. We've mentioned a lot of designers by name in this book, and while it's possible you're familiar with all of them, it's also possible you're wondering, "Who are all these people, and why—or how—should I get to know them?" This is where you'll have to do a little bit of work, but luckily that "work" is much easier now than it's ever been before. It's also more fun.

Once upon a time, if you wanted to discover or get to know the work of a contemporary designer, you would've had to do one or more of the following:

- Buy or borrow a pile of shelter and design magazines, like *Architectural Digest* or *Domus* or *Nest*

- Travel to New York to go to a design store like the now-closed but once-legendary Moss

- Fly to Milan to attend Salone del Mobile, the annual international furniture fair

- Be an architect or designer who had access to appointment-only showrooms

- Hire an architect or designer to source contemporary furniture for you

Now, of course, it's simply a matter of hopping online. The problem is, there's so much information online that it can be dizzying to navigate it all and find your own way in. But try to remember that if you're just trying to orient yourself and get to know key players, the stakes are pretty low: "You don't have to buy anything to be involved in the design community, particularly on Instagram," says Alhadeff. A great place to start on Instagram is by digging deeper into the profile of a design publication you like, or a cool design store or gallery, or an interior designer or stylist who often sources pieces by contemporary makers. We've also had good luck discovering designers by clicking through to profiles when galleries repost the creative crowds who attend their openings, and by scouring the designer lists from group exhibitions, which often include both established talents and some we've never heard of.

We follow a ton of designers as a way to keep up a steady stream of story subjects, yes, but also as a way to stay inspired, and as a way to participate in an online dialogue with the design community. Even if you're new to this, you can participate, too—if you see an object by a designer you like on Instagram, don't just follow them. Comment on their posts. Participate in their polls. Some designers, like Lily and Hopie Stockman, the sisters who run the boutique LA textiles brand Block Shop, even invite their followers into the design process in this way, asking things like, "Which pattern do you like better for this scarf?" Or, "What color would you prefer as an upholstery fabric?" It's an easy way to get involved and deepen your connection with the contemporary work you admire, before (or after) you invest in it.

Another way to look for inspiration is by going out and seeing design in person, which we find is the most valuable way to get a sense of materials and proportions, especially if you're actually thinking about buying something. Of course, this isn't always possible, and we've had great luck buying things online, sight unseen—no pun intended. But if you can get out and about, here are a few different places you can consider.

Nylon Telephone by Philippe Malouin for Salon 94 Design, 2019

● GALLERIES

Design galleries typically traffic in high-end one-offs and limited editions, made by designers who have a proven track record of selling to collectors. While we often can't afford most of what's on view, galleries can be a great place to learn about different materials, get a sense of scale, and generally get inspired in the same way you would visiting an art museum or browsing a high-end fashion boutique. If you live in a city with a good contemporary design gallery—such as Volume Gallery in Chicago, Side Gallery in Barcelona, SEEDS in London, Etage Projects in Copenhagen, or Friedman Benda in New York—it's worth subscribing to the gallery's newsletter to find out when openings are happening. Like art openings, design openings are always free and open to the public. Get there early, so you can actually see the objects on view and talk to the designers who made them. If you don't know what kinds of questions to ask, go with Sight Unseen's three most basic queries: (1) What inspired you to make this piece? (2) How did you make it? (3) Can you tell me more about the materials you used? Don't ask the designer how much the piece costs; at galleries, there's typically a price sheet if you inquire at the front desk. And if you can't make the opening, try to visit another day. It's such a different experience seeing objects in person.

● SHOWROOMS

Showrooms are similar to galleries in that you generally can't walk in off the street and buy, say, a housewarming gift for your most design-savvy friend. But they're different because they do away with the idea of scarcity, typically featuring unlimited editions of furniture and lighting, made to order by the designers or brands they represent. We often use showrooms like galleries—i.e., places to stop in from time to time for inspiration—but if you're thinking of investing in a pricier piece, these are great places to visit as well. Some of our favorites include Egg Collective, Love House, and Roll & Hill in New York; Atelier de Troupe in Los Angeles; Modern Times in Melbourne; Spartan Shop in Portland; and Jermaine Gallacher in London. We would also consider places like MATTER, The Future Perfect, and London's Monologue in this category.

Geology Table 03 by Chen Chen & Kai Williams for The Future Perfect, 2019

● DESIGN STORES

There are so many different kinds of design stores—big ones, like Hay in Copenhagen or Merci in Paris, and small ones, like YOWIE in Philadelphia, Arranging Things in Stockholm, or Kollekted By in Oslo. There are design stores in people's homes, like Casa Ahorita in Mexico City, and design stores in people's restaurants, like RW Guild in New York. Some of the best design stores are in museums, like SHOP Cooper Hewitt or—the mother of them all—MoMA Design Store. These are often the sweet spot for actually buying more available and affordable objects, and this is where it can be just as effective to shop online as in person, for the sheer breadth of offerings. One site we often use when searching for design objects is Garmentory, because it aggregates small boutiques across North America that we might not have otherwise visited on our Internet rounds. It's also always fun to locate the cool design store in any city you're visiting, as these are often the places where you'll find objects by local makers.

● DESIGN FAIRS

As design professionals, we often attend furniture fairs like ICFF in New York, or Salone del Mobile in Milan, which take place in large conference halls and are meant for members of the design trade to see (and order) the newest launches from brands and studios. We wouldn't recommend that non-professionals attend these kinds of trade fairs, but there are usually smaller exhibitions and events around town during these fairs that are more relevant for your average design lover. They're often organized by the designers themselves or by local curators, and they can be great places for discovery, as they tend to feature a lot of new work by up-and-coming designers (who are often, as a bonus, on hand to chat about their inspirations). As part of those events, there are also sometimes opportunities to buy objects you might never have seen otherwise. One of Jill's most prized possessions is a mustard-colored frosted glass vase by Swedish designer Jonatan Nilsson, which she snagged from an Arranging Things pop-up happening in a women's boutique during Stockholm Design Week. She found it when she went out shopping for a hat!

At the end of the day, you can absolutely do all of your looking and learning from the comfort of your own home. But there's also so much to be gained by seeing objects in person and speaking to the humans whose work went into their making. We can't tell you the number of times we've discovered that a piece was much larger or smaller than it appeared in photos, shinier or less reflective, dinkily made or incredibly well resolved—or heard its incredible backstory, which we might never have known if we were just scrolling past it on Instagram.

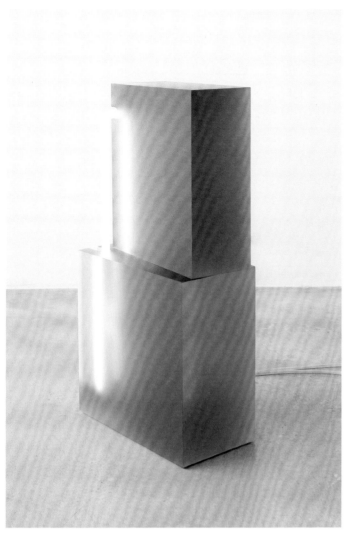

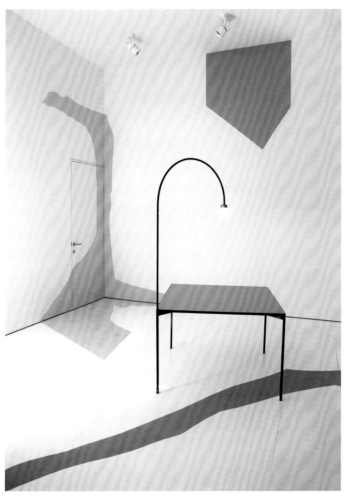

opposite: 3D Collage Table Green by Kiki Van Eijk for Spazio Nobile Gallery, 2021

above left: Totem light by Sabine Marcelis, 2021

above right: BTM Ceramics 2101 vessel by Philipp Schenk-Mischke, 2021

left: Table + Lamp by Muller Van Severen, 2011

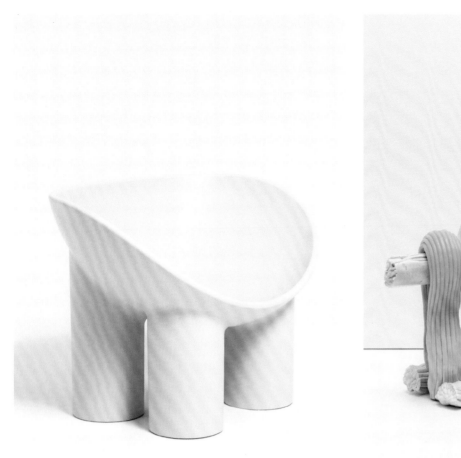

above left: Roly-Poly Chair by Toogood, 2014

above right: Recycled plastic baroque toilet paper holder by James Shaw, 2013

right: Hard round bench by Soft Baroque for Patrick Parrish Gallery, 2016

opposite: Supportive chair by Luam Melake for R & Company, 2021

SHOPPING

In the art world, if an artist is represented by a gallery, that gallery is often the only place from which you can acquire their work. In the design world, representation by galleries exists, but the boundaries are often more fluid and opportunities to own a small piece of an important designer's work abound. For example, New York designer Misha Kahn sells his car paint–covered resin mirrors for five figures through Friedman Benda. But he also sells $28 glass straws through retailers such as Mociun and Coming Soon. This underscores an important thing to know about contemporary objects: While a gallery object—which is typically made by hand in small, collectible editions—usually costs much more than a production object that's made in a factory, some of the best designers have been known to create both, and you can definitely find great artistry and great value in both places.

So, if you dream of owning a piece by Chen Chen & Kai Williams but can't afford their made-to-order coffee table at The Future Perfect, for example, you can always start with the $90 ceramic planter they designed for the affordable gift brand Areaware. If you can't stop saving images of Sabine Marcelis's candy-colored resin cubes, yet can't stomach their $4,000 price tag, maybe you can scratch that itch by buying one of the equally colorful but less expensive poufs she created for the Swedish design brand Hem. And there are some designers you can find at almost every scale and price point. Take the Belgian duo Muller Van Severen.

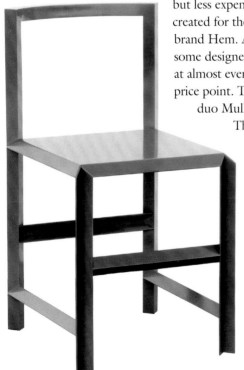

They're best known for their expensive hybrid furniture, like powder-coated steel shelves attached to low-slung leather seats, or tables connected to floor lamps.

But they also make kitchens for Reform, flatware and salt shakers for Valerie Objects, $145 vases for Hay, and sofas for a Belgian fashion brand called KASSL. If you're a fan of their work, you're likely to find a piece by them in your price range.

Sometimes the same piece can even drop dramatically in price if a designer licenses it to a more mass-market company. For instance, when London-based designer Faye Toogood debuted her iconic, chubby-legged Roly Poly chair, she first designed versions in fiberglass, resin, aluminum, and even liquid barium crystal. These were made by hand by master artisans and priced accordingly; one, made from sand-cast bronze and silver nitrate, topped out at $45,000. While those versions are still for sale, Toogood eventually licensed the design to the Italian company Driade, which manufactures a more affordable version of Roly Poly in polyethylene—a fancy word for plastic—that's made using an industrial process known as rotational molding. At $790, it's still expensive, but comparatively speaking, it's a steal, and has become wildly popular as a result.

Toogood's chair brings up an important thing to understand about shopping for contemporary objects, which is why things cost the way they do (a topic also commonly known as "A sofa costs how much?!?"). Sometimes, even items that are referred to as "accessible" can still cost what seems like a lot of money. That's because when you buy a designer-made object, you aren't just paying for labor and materials, though some materials are inherently more expensive, such as bronze or marble. You're also paying for the years of education and training it took for the designer to get where they are.

Elle Chair by Marco Campardo, 2020

You're paying for research and development costs, as so many designers are inventing or reinventing fabrication processes. Sometimes you're paying a premium for an object that's made nearby, to sustain a local economy; sometimes you're paying more so that artisans overseas can make a living wage. So many unseen factors go into pricing contemporary work before you even get to its perceptual value, which is the value that's attached to certain designers who have a proven ability for sales in the market. "The reality is, most of the objects I'm interested in are made by hand by a young artist in their studio, and they're spending hours, days, months, or even years on this object," says Zoe Fisher, director of Salon 94 design gallery. "These objects are a labor of love and time and effort and education, and that's why they cost so much."

As for sofas? Sofas are expensive for some of the same reasons—they're not easily made on a factory assembly line, and often require much skilled work by hand. But sofas are also priced higher because there's no way to manufacture them affordably in small quantities, unlike, say, a glass vase. They either require very expensive hand labor in a small workshop, when made in small batches, or huge minimum quantities when made in a factory, which requires a gigantic up-front investment and financial risk (hundreds of thousands of dollars, as opposed to a couple thousand for the glass vase). Also, since they're physically larger, they require much more complex and expensive infrastructure to ship, store, and sell. This is why items like beds and sofas aren't as frequently made by independent design studios as, say, chairs or small home goods.

We've talked a lot about why things are expensive, but there are also plenty of contemporary objects that are within reach, even beyond the smaller production items we mentioned earlier. "We can't all live with everything unique and handmade, and now, there are so many companies that fit between the Ikea budget and the gallery budget," says Gilbert, referring to brands such as Dims., Hay, Hem, and more. However, unlike vintage, there isn't an obvious secondary market for contemporary design—aka where to find a Toogood chair or an Eny Lee Parker lamp that's been gently used—aside from sites like Craigslist, Chairish, and Facebook Marketplace. But there are other ways to find deals on new or used contemporary objects if you know where to look. Here are a few of our favorites.

● STUDIO SALES, SAMPLE SALES, AND SECONDS SALES

We've already explained why it's a good idea to follow your favorite makers and brands on social media, but here's another reason: Many designers, especially those who make small goods like ceramics and glass, hold studio or seconds sales on a seasonal basis. Here, you'll often find like-new pieces with barely noticeable nicks or other manufacturing defects, prototypes, or funny material experiments that didn't make it to market—all for a discount. Other studios, like Peter Shire's Echo Park Pottery in Los Angeles, use holiday sales as a way to offload a ton of new work at once. We've even known bigger companies like Knoll, Vitra, and Fritz Hansen to hold semiannual sales. Of course, these can be city-specific, but we've also heard of designers putting their sale items online if there's enough customer demand—so don't be afraid to ask!

● DESIGN-SCHOOL SALES

It also pays to keep an eye on design schools' social media accounts or newsletters. The Ceramics Program at Harvard, for example, holds a weekend exhibition and sale of planters and other student work twice a year, while Cranbrook Academy of Art's ceramics program also holds a yearly mug sale. It's a great way to buy an affordable piece from an up-and-coming talent before they hit it big—and the price of their work quadruples.

● CHARITY AUCTIONS AND RAFFLES

The Instagram charity auction and raffle has low-key become our favorite place to snag new work you couldn't otherwise afford. Yes, nine times out of ten you won't win, but it's often a smaller pool of entries than you think, and either way, your money goes to a good cause. Monica's won prizes in fundraiser raffles twice now—including a caned stool by up-and-coming London designer Elliot Barnes—so you never know.

● WRIGHT NOW

Wright auction house in Chicago is mostly known for its sales of high-end mid-century and contemporary items (and for things absolutely smoking their estimates, like a Gio Ponti glassware set that sold for $32,000 back in 2019). But a lesser-known arm called Wright Now offers a buy-it-now function for both vintage and new items, and while not everything is affordable, it's a way to know exactly what you're signing up for, especially when compared to the auction format. Wright's midsummer Mass Modern auction also typically includes some contemporary design lots. These auctions are notable because there's no reserve—meaning there's no minimum price the auction house needs to hit before the piece sells—which makes it a good place to find a deal.

● THE HERMAN MILLER COMPANY STORE AND DESIGN WITHIN REACH OUTLETS

An increasing number of design brands in America fall under the umbrella of the massive furniture manufacturer Herman Miller—including Knoll, DWR, Muuto, and Hay—which means that an increasing number of those items can be found at the company's outlet stores, including two DWR outlets in the New York City area and a Herman Miller Company Store that sells both online and at the company's headquarters in Zeeland, Michigan.

● BARTERING

This isn't something we'd recommend when you're first blindly reaching out to a designer. But if you're a creative person who makes a physical product or offers a service that might be valuable to a designer, there's no harm in suggesting a trade once you've established a rapport. Just don't be pushy about it if they politely decline.

Perhaps the most important shopping tip we can offer is this: In the same way that you might keep browsing the latest collections by your favorite fashion designers in the middle of a pandemic, when you're not leaving the house, if you're serious about filling your home with amazing contemporary design, it's better to always be on the lookout for objects that move you, rather than only looking when you need to tick specific items off a shopping list. "If you go out and shop for mugs, it's less exciting to me than when you happen to encounter one and think, 'I have to have this,'" says Gilbert. "If you buy things that 'fit the list,' you won't achieve that layered, authentic feeling of you. Great design isn't always available immediately when you want it, and sometimes you have to, when you see it, jump."

above: The Paradise Light by Roxanne Ferreira, Arrange Studio, 2021
opposite: Kink Vase by Earnest Studio for Muuto, 2018

opposite: Office sconce by Elliot Barnes, 2021

above left: Barbar Series table lamp by Studio Anne Holtrop for Maniera, 2018

above right: Jupiter's Lounge Chair by Mac Collins for The New Craftsmen, 2021

right: Lawn & Tennis Chair by Sam Stewart, 2019

BUYING

So how do you know when to jump? What factors should you consider before actually making a purchase? As we mentioned before, there's the all-important emotional aspect—how an object makes you feel just by looking at it. "A combination of wit and humor is always appreciated, with an understanding of technique and materials that I haven't seen before," says Fisher. "And even if I have seen it before, it has to be something that gives me that warm and fuzzy feeling." But gut instinct counts for more than just warm fuzzies in the long run; it actually helps make your purchases more sustainable. You'll hold on to a piece you really love for longer than you will a piece that simply checks a box, no matter how cool it is or how great it looks in your Instagram vignettes. Alhadeff agrees: "Whether you buy it at CB2 or The Future Perfect or Carpenters Workshop Gallery, or you bid on it at auction, you have a responsibility to have a real fundamental desire for that thing, and not just be using it to fill a hole in your house temporarily while you wait for something else."

Sometimes, if the desire is strong enough, you might even buy a piece that has no obvious destination in your interior, and resolve to figure out where to place it, or how to use it, later. For instance, Jill once bought a pendant light that she loved but had nowhere to put, carrying it around to two different apartments before eventually finding the perfect spot for it. (Of course it was flat-packed, which made the whole endeavor a bit easier.) Chairs are almost always a decent investment, because if you find one you love, you can put it pretty much anywhere you please—in an entryway, at the end of a hall, next to a credenza. You don't have to spring for a set of four or six around a dining table, and you don't even have to use it for seating—Monica likes to keep a chair in her bedroom to use as a valet for clothes she's taken off or plans to wear the next day. Sometimes chairs can simply be visual accents, too.

Of course, beyond just having enough space, there are often many more practical concerns to consider when deciding whether a piece of contemporary design is worth acquiring, especially when the item is handmade in a studio by an independent designer rather than produced in a factory by a design brand. This is where the three M's—materials, maker, and market research—come into play yet again, albeit in a slightly different way.

Materials

In general, contemporary designers tend to work with materials in one of three different ways, and whether an object's material story affects your purchase, what kinds of resources went into an object's making is valuable information to understand. First, there are designers who work with traditional materials—like wood, brass, aluminum, onyx, glass, or marble—using relatively traditional fabrication processes, like woodworking or glassblowing. Some of our favorite designers in this category include Fort Standard, Waka Waka, Egg Collective, Mark Grattan, Green River Project, and Vonnegut/Kraft, among so many more. The beauty of their work often lies in the rigorous design and in the playful or otherwise thoughtfully executed modern details.

Then there are designers who use traditional materials in experimental ways, aided by the use of contemporary technologies or innovatively adapted processes, much like Alvar Aalto and the Eameses did when they reinvented the silhouette of plywood simply by bending it. Today's designers often use computer-controlled tools to achieve their desired look, like the Copenhagen-based duo Wang & Söderström, whose ceramics are 3D-printed, or Guatemalan designer Giovanni Valdeavellano of Studio POA, whose wooden tables are CNC-milled using hand-drawn forms harnessed from an iPad. These kinds of designs also include those based on the appropriation of industrial techniques, like ceramic extrusion—a process once used primarily for pipe-building in infrastructure projects. It has recently been adapted at the studio level by designers like Anton Alvarez and Floris Wubben to create something akin to art.

Finally, there are designers who have moved past creating with existing techniques entirely and have begun inventing their own. As we mentioned above, we believe that this is the defining story of twenty-first-century design, and is thus one of the most sought-after themes in contemporary collecting; it's certainly the thread that seems to run through most work at the gallery level. One of our favorite designers in this category is the London-based Philipp Schenk-Mischke, who uses a body vibration plate—the kind you might find at the gym—to jiggle his ceramics into a gently slumping form. Another is the Indiana-based designer Christopher Stuart, who purposefully introduces glitches into his normally precise design software in order to arrive at his tables' slightly off-kilter silhouettes. Some practitioners have even invented new materials, including the Dutch-based Dirk van der Kooij, who makes colorful, swirling tables from the melted-down remnants of reclaimed compact discs, and Jongjin Park, who paints thin sheets of paper towel with clay slip, layers them like pastry dough, then fires the resulting object in a kiln to achieve the hardness of ceramics.

In terms of how these different approaches should affect your potential purchase, in many cases, they won't (though they do make for amazing dinner party conversations!). But understanding the differences between them is still a part of doing due diligence to get to know exactly what it is you're buying, and whether it's worth buying. You're not going to go wrong with something made from natural materials, both in terms of value and longevity, because natural materials

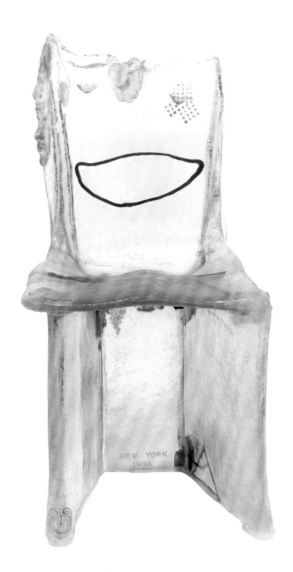

often age well, even when they develop a patina, and they're easily repaired or refinished if damaged. Newer materials—like recycled fabrics, paper pulp, or foam—don't have the benefit of time to see how they'll age, but these materials are often lacquered or otherwise preserved to increase their life span. And plastic, while sometimes prone to discoloration over time, is virtually indestructible—not exactly a selling point when purchasing new, sustainably speaking, but a plus when the material in question is recycled.

Of course, if you're buying a piece that's made from an unusual or otherwise untested material, it's always a risk—one that you'll have to assess in terms of the price you're paying for it versus the pleasure you'll feel from having such an interesting conversation piece in your home. But at the end of the day, it's smart to invest in a piece of contemporary design that's been made by hand in a studio because it will typically last longer and be more valuable than something mass produced, as long as it's cared for. "There's no one material that's the best investment," Alhadeff agrees. "If the structure is good, high-quality work made in most materials will last and age well. And anything that can carry the story of your life with the object is an incredible thing to buy for the long term, you know?"

opposite: Pete & Nora Floor Lamp by Egg Collective, 2016

above: Pratt Chair #7 1984/2018 (Light Blue) by Gaetano Pesce for Salon 94 Design, 2018, courtesy of the artist and Salon 94 Design

left: Anodized aluminum coffee table by Fredrik Paulsen for Etage Projects, 2017

Maker

When you're buying design, one consideration is whether a piece will appreciate, or at least retain its value over time. One way to ensure this is to only buy items that are authentic and can be easily traced back to the designers who made them. Yep, we're talking about knockoffs, which can be a complicated and prickly subject. Some people justify knockoffs as making design more democratic and accessible to people at all economic levels. They also argue, when it comes to copies of vintage pieces by long-dead designers like Eileen Gray or Jean Royère, that the originals are too scarce and hard to come by. But when it comes to contemporary objects made by living designers, this view doesn't take into account the emotional and financial toll that knockoffs can have on the designer who's been copied. "Knockoffs are taking away a person's access to their own idea and stripping them of ownership of their concept," says Alhadeff. "When someone engages in knocking off a contemporary designer in a flagrant way, they are, in a sense, taking a bit of that person. The people who knock off just see a business opportunity. But it's something buyers should be more conscientious of, because the truth is that our legal system doesn't protect ideas."

Identifying knockoffs in the current landscape can be difficult, because they're so widespread and not everyone has an encyclopedic knowledge of the more small-batch works that are typically targeted. Contemporary knockoffs can be anything from big brands mimicking a form developed by an independent designer (which can be especially financially crushing) to interior designers stealthily having a piece fabricated more cheaply in a workshop rather than purchasing it from the actual maker. There are also certain Internet retailers whose entire business plan is based around making and selling knockoffs. Generally the most telltale sign of a knockoff is the price. If we search "Eny Lee Parker Oo Lamp," we get results for the real thing, which costs around $4,000 on 1stDibs. But we're also served something that looks identical—because copycats will also often use a designer's own product photography—for $170 from a place called Vakkerlight. If you spot something with a really strong design language that seems too cheap to be true, there's a decent chance it probably is.

We have a relatively simple view of knockoffs, which is that they're never worth it. In addition to the fact that they hold no resale value and will be worthless to future generations, their very existence goes against the core lesson of this book! You'll never feel emotionally fulfilled by buying a piece that was the result of theft.

Market research

The contemporary design market is not unlike the contemporary art market, in that there are important pieces that sell at auction for huge sums of money. Its first boom was in 2010, when the British designer Marc Newson famously sold a prototype of his 1990 Lockheed Lounge chair for more than a million dollars. More recently, Max Lamb stands out in terms of the appreciation of his work. "A pewter chair that Max made in 2006 cost £1,000 then, and now it's like £40,000," Dzekciorius points out. But while it's good to look to the market to understand whether the price you're considering paying for a piece is fair, based on the designer's other work or based on the category it falls into, all of the design experts we spoke to recommended against buying contemporary design primarily as a financial investment—in part because it's very difficult to identify who's going to reach stratospheric heights when they're just starting out. Those same experts all had stories of their own radars misfiring—times when they had the opportunity to purchase a piece by a designer before they became huge, but didn't. "The first time I saw Takuro Kuwata's ceramics, I had a sucker-punch reaction to how amazing his work was," says Gilbert. "It felt too expensive at the time, but I look back on it and I'm like, now I'm *really* not going to be able to afford a piece. I blew it."

opposite: Ecco mirror by Barber Osgerby for Glas Italia, 2018

above: Serpentine Chair by Chris Schanck for Reyes | Finn, 2020

A different way to buy

Buying merely as a financial investment—or because "everyone's got a Max Lamb now, so I need one too"—also runs counter to our idea of acquiring items because you have an aesthetic or emotional affinity for them. But if you have your heart set on owning a unique collectible by a certain maker, there is one way to do it that's a lot more personal: Commissioning something custom—whether it's asking a designer to rework an existing piece in a new color, material, or size, or hiring them to create something new entirely because you simply love their work—is, in some respects, the ultimate way to create an emotional attachment to the objects in your home. It's a rewarding process that results in a piece that's completely unique to you, and it can even foster a special relationship between you and the designer. For example, Jill recently commissioned a desk from New York designer Jonah Takagi. Not only does the desk look perfect in her home and fulfill a genuine need—WFH for life, she needs the storage space its two columns of drawers offers—but it also serves as a daily reminder of the summer she and Takagi spent talking on the phone, refining the desk's details, and working together to create something beautiful.

Custom work—particularly furniture—isn't cheap, and it comes with its own set of challenges. We spoke to New York designer Sam Stewart, who works primarily on commission; he explained, "I think people are at first enthused about it, and then they sometimes cool off when I walk them through what things cost, what shipping and crating may or may not cost, and all that other logistical stuff. And then also letting people know the truth, which is—especially if it's a one-off design— we're talking about a six-month lead time, minimum."

If you're serious about commissioning a piece, a good approach might be to set up a studio visit to see the quality of work in person, and to talk through some of those issues. Design has always been a generally transparent industry, and there are often studio email addresses listed on a designer's website. Instagram is also your friend here: "Social media

has stripped away a lot of the intimidating process," says Fisher. "You can pick out a designer that you like and slide into their DMs. If that designer is represented by a gallery, then they'll connect you to the gallery, but I think most designers would be very excited to get a direct message and have the conversation." Gilbert agrees: "Starting a dialogue can be as easy as just saying, 'I really admire your work,' and seeing where it takes you. It could lead to a studio visit, or an in-person meetup, or a conversation about what they might make for you, or what availability there is for something they have. There's no reason to be timid, at least in striking up a conversation and feeling it out."

The appeal of the new

If we're being honest, contemporary objects might be the most difficult genre in this book to collect. They can be expensive, they can take a long time to produce, and they can sometimes feel *too* shiny and new (buy only contemporary objects, and your home could end up looking like a sterile modern showroom, or an overly trendy influencer apartment). But in the end, they're truly exciting to have in your home, sparking thoughts and conversations about new materials, new aesthetics, and new talents—some of whom may even be your peers. They're also highly rewarding as well, filled with stories about the life you lived, the time you lived it in, and the artisans you met or admired along the way. While buying vintage is about appreciating someone else's history, buying contemporary is about documenting your own, and if you get to support the creativity of others as you're doing it, it can feel all the more worth it.

opposite: EN 312 Shelves by Haus Otto, 2021
above left: Dou Floor Lamp by Ferm Living, 2021
above: Kosa Side Chair by Ian Felton, 2019

HELENA BARQUET & FABIANA FARIA

Since founding their popular Lower East Side housewares shop Coming Soon in 2013, **Barquet and Faria** have become known for championing emerging design talents and for making a slew of vintage and kitsch objects relevant for a contemporary audience. That passion extends to their personal lives, too. There's almost nothing contemporary in their Rockaway Beach bungalow—a former German swim club that dates back to 1910—that isn't made by a designer they carry in their shop.

"Most people would assume that our house would be like the store—concrete floors, white walls, glass. Not a wood cabin. So, it was exciting for us to think about our things in this context. We both love French mid-century furniture and Italian lighting, and we draw inspiration from those eras. But then it becomes its own thing, which is very much what Coming Soon is about. Coming Soon has become its own aesthetic."

" The corn stool by Third Drawer Down is a special piece. Like a lot of things in the store, we were hesitant about it at first, but then it ended up being a staple. There are these plastic Chinatown stools that we use as stepstools, and the corn is a more fun version of that stool. We can move it around really easily, or step on it, and it's just fine. It's a hilarious piece. The bite is everything."

"We're surrounded by so many contemporary objects that people are surprised when things are vintage. It's because we're drawn to pieces that are timeless and the romantic notion that when things are made well, they get to have really long lives. We reupholster a lot, and our choice of color often makes a vintage piece look contemporary. The couch, for example, we ended up reupholstering in this punchy orange-sherbet velvet. Sometimes you start with a color that seems sort of wild, but the minute it comes into your home, it becomes a highlight. There's no way you're missing a giant orange poufy sofa." ←

"Concrete Cat is a lovely Canadian design studio that we've worked with for what seems like forever. They were on our mood board when we opened the store. Each time their pieces arrive, it feels like Christmas, because each one is different. You get this very emotional feeling toward one color or another, and that particular ashtray just spoke to us. The orange Cassie Griffin tray we got on the street when Dimes was having a little sale during COVID. Bright colors in general are always really important in the mix." ↑

" The Vaseline-glass plates from Mosser on our shelves is one of the most exciting things that we've gotten to do. Mosser has been family-owned since the 1950s, and the designs are from the original molds. Vaseline glass was something that they weren't allowed to keep doing in the '80s because it contains uranium. But they found this old stock of Vaseline glass chips, so they made us a small run. When it's gone, it's gone. It will be a true collectible item. And again, it looks so contemporary even though it's an old design."

" Because the house was once a German swim club, the living room was one big open space. We were interested in making it feel more intimate; neither of us has a major lust for loft living. Cold Picnic helped us create the wall-to-wall carpet, and that already helped cut up so much of the space. There were too many woods! The carpet really grounded it."

66 Our love for objects goes hand in hand with the people who make them. It's a great luxury that we get to be friends with Phoebe and Peter from Cold Picnic, or F. Taylor Colantonio, or Concrete Cat, or Katie Stout, who made the little blue lamp in our guest room. But even to be in the same generation as these designers, and to get to follow their careers—you become much more invested in the things they make. It's a big part of why design has grown so much."

66 The Fredericks and Mae cutting boards are made from these run-of-the-mill industrial chopping blocks that chefs usually have—different colors for each thing that they cook, so, like, a poultry one, a vegetable one, a beef. Fredericks and Mae use the material that's leftover when they route out the cutting boards. It's genius, and it's indestructible. We sound like an infomercial, but we put it out so often as a serving piece when we entertain, and people always want to touch it, and they're interested in how it's made." →

At home with
MARK GRATTAN

Grattan's work is moody, smoky, sensual, and chic—all qualities that, a few years back, earned him first prize on the television show *Ellen's Next Great Designer*. His Mexico City apartment, on the fourth floor of a building by famed architect Luis Barragán, has a similar vibe, filled with black leather, velvet, wall-to-wall carpeting, and sleek, low pieces designed by Grattan himself.

" In my living room [previous spread], there's a black gridded candleholder by EWE studio. The white sandy sculpture in the center of the coffee table is by Pablo Arellano from Studio IMA, and the red vase is by Bertrand Fompeyrine from Chic by Accident. The ashtray is from when I was doing my research on glass fabrication.

Inside the coffee table is the inspiration for one of the first pieces I did, a table called Café Con Leche. I found this sculpture at the Lagunilla flea market, and it has been with me for all of these years. When I started putting the apartment together, I sprayed it white and put it behind bronze glass. It sits with me as a reminder of and an homage to that first piece." →

" When I moved into this apartment, I lived in it empty for about fourteen months. One of the things I noticed most about the space was the travel of light throughout the day. The building is not high, but it sits above the tree line across from a park in Colonia San Rafael. In general, lighting is one of the first things people need to think about in a space—not just the natural light, but how you place lighting within a home. For me, it was a lot of thrift shopping, except for two Apparatus pieces—a sconce in the bedroom, and a pendant in the living room. Apparatus is something I don't see in Mexico, but it works with the Mexican aesthetic. The material palette is very warm, and the simplicity of shapes works well. Apparatus founder Gabriel Hendifar's use of repetition is something that I'm attracted to and that I use a lot in my work."

"I've designed a lot of beds. I'm always thinking about a bed, and I'm not even a heavy sleeper! I'm up very early in the morning. I can't take naps. Maybe I'm attracted to the form because there's an inherent challenge in the scale. It's so big, and these things are typically so cumbersome."

"In my living room, the blue vase and purple sculpture by Bertrand Fompeyrine help warm things up. I like to use other people's objects as a balance to the rigidity in my work." ← →

"The green cabinet in the living room is custom. It's lined inside with mirror, and the faces are upholstered in monochromatic green velvet to match everything else in the room. The double hardware on the outside gives it a little swag, and the marble matches the velvet. I actually dyed the marble green. To me, the cabinet is about the cleanliness of repetition. It gives a sense of order. So, everything is repetitive in one way or another in this room. The mirrors. The cabinet. The two sofas. The sconces. Even the piece of sculpture in the base of the coffee table and the Candle Grids by EWE in the living room are just a repetition of shape." →

I love the brutality of this chrome vase by Tomás Díaz Cedeño. I can see his hand in it, which is nice because everything in my space is so clean. The chrome sconces on the mirror are my favorite part of the room. They're from the Lagunilla flea market, and they have little cat eyes that open up. They're so sleazy; there's something almost sinister about them. In my work and in my home, I feel like I'm channeling something I can't necessarily channel in real life, which is this provocation, this sexuality, this outspokenness, this sort of luxe that I'm attracted to, but can't communicate through a vehicle other than furniture. I couldn't walk down the street communicating these things, even with what I wear. But I can communicate it with my hand and through the work."

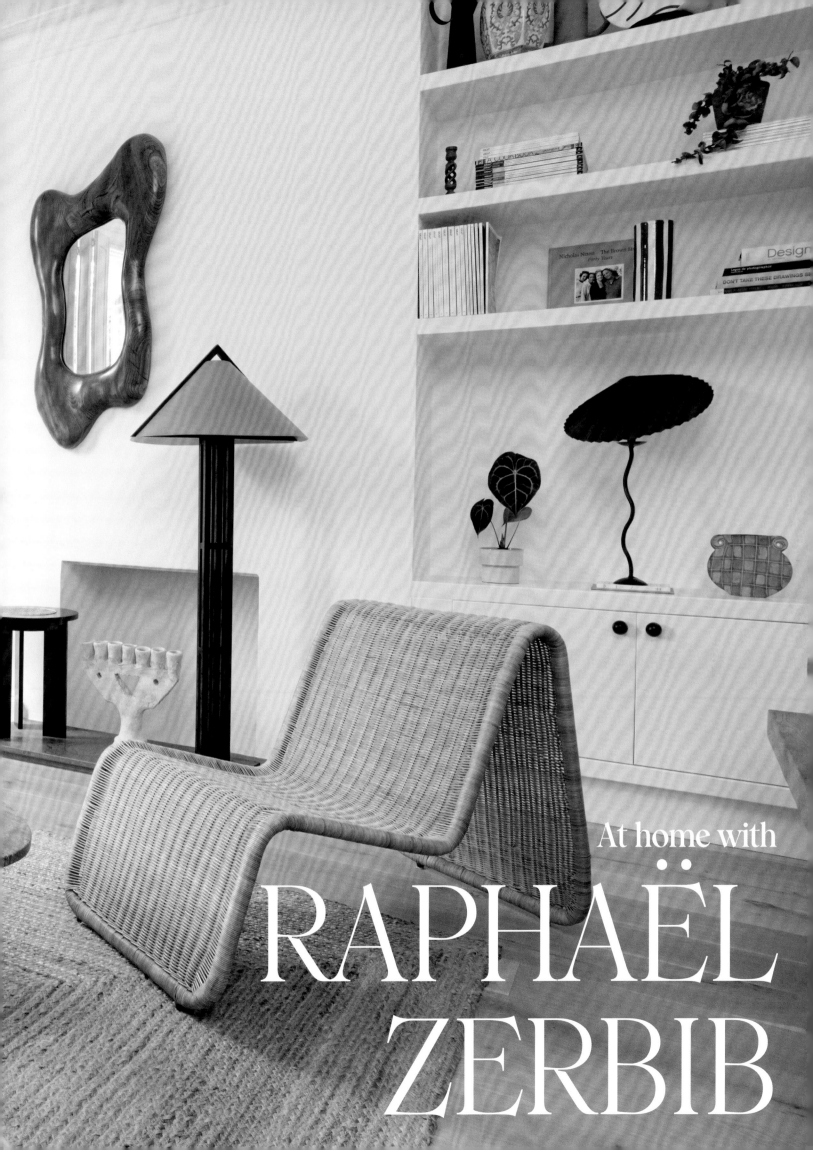

At home with
RAPHAËL
ZERBÏB

Though he works as a quantitative analyst for a bank, spending his days creating computer programs and mathematical models, Toulouse-born **Zerbib** always had an itch to create in a more artistic way. Once he moved to London and bought his first apartment—which he shares with his husband, Julian, and their dog—he began conceiving his own furniture and collaborating with artisans, fabricators, and designers like Elliot Barnes to bring it to life.

" My approach to design has evolved a lot from back when I was only worshiping the Memphis style. I like mixing styles from different eras or different designers, and I like mixing antiques and contemporary pieces. They can tell a different story than if they're placed apart, and for me, it's the right way to make design history relevant—to make the past, present, and future talk to each other through objects."

" The desk I designed. I liked the idea of the legs appearing to traverse the desktop and the seat of the chair. I drew the shape—I keep a sketchbook for ideas—and asked a woodworker to carve it for me. I've always been attracted to creation. My job is very cerebral, and while it's fulfilling, the ability to create something by hand, and the freedom of that, is missing from what I do, so throughout the years I kept feeding this passion. Because I have ideas, I can work with people who can help me to create my own furniture, and that's been rewarding for me." ←

"My husband and I made the headboard completely with our bare hands. It was a challenge. I've designed many things, but before this I'd never participated in the manufacturing process, so for me this was the next level, making something from scratch. The only thing we didn't do ourselves was get the shape cut out of plywood, but we drew the shape. I liked how the vase looks like it's cut out of paper. You can't really put flowers or water in it, and it's not really symmetrical; I like that it's imperfect."

" We got these plates when we were traveling on holidays in Puglia, in a village called Grottaglie that has a bunch of ceramic artists living there." ↑

" The mirror is one of my favorite pieces. I found the woodworker who made it, Christophe Daguet, on Instagram, and fell in love with this mirror. It's imperfect, but at the same time it's really beautifully made; when you get closer you can see that the grain isn't exactly how it's supposed to be everywhere, or there are bits of inlaid wood that help hold it together. So, you see the hand work behind it, which is something I really value." ↑

"I'm really drawn to lamps that have this typical lamp shape, but revisited. Like this Oscar Piccolo one with the leg and pleated shade, or the dining room pendant lamp. The only exception is the Memphis lamps; they're more like objects for me that I collect. And they have a meaning for me, because Memphis is something I discovered very early, when I was at university, and it made me aware that when you're a designer, you can make amazing, funny, beautiful things, and that's how you learn to create a living interior that's specific to you and not dictated by trends." →

"The dining room lamp is by Elliot Barnes, and the idea was to have this big, fat, squared pyramid sitting on top of the table. The table is also by Elliot. The painting is by my husband. It's supposed to be my husband, his best friend, and her dog. I wanted something that represented a usual dinner scene and Julian—who's a fashion stylist—said, 'I can do it, because I used to paint before.' I didn't trust him at the beginning, but in the end, I loved it so much. It's a great piece of art."

The coffee table I designed with Elliot Barnes. The inspiration behind it is a ceramic steak I bought from Astier de Villatte (shown in the previous spread). It's one of my husband's favorite objects, and he suggested the idea. Elliot likes to name the pieces he makes, and the name of this table is Bavette, the Glacier, and a Silver Room. The painting over the sofa is by Jason Tessier. I have a few paintings of his, but I particularly like this one because when I look at it, I always see an upside-down face. I like that it allows you the opportunity to decide what it represents to you. Anyone looking at it will have a different interpretation. The wavy floor lamp is by Gary Morga." ←

We found these two paintings at a charity shop for twenty pounds, but they were really dirty, so you couldn't really see the colors. We cleaned them by looking at videos on the Internet, and now we really like them. The console table I designed, and it represents my obsession with waves. It's a little bit of a trick—it's made of plywood, but it's covered with oak veneer. And I always dreamed of having this Michele De Lucchi lamp, so it's one of the first pieces I bought once I could afford it." ↓

146

RODMAN PRIMACK & RUDY WEISSEN-BERG

Primack and Weissenberg are all over the map, both literally—with houses in Guatemala, Mexico City, and New York—and figuratively, with multiple professional interests that ultimately converge around contemporary design. Primack is a former director of Design Miami and currently runs the textile and interiors studio RP Miller, while Weissenberg, a former television exec, now works in real estate development. Together, the pair founded the design gallery AGO Projects, which is just a short drive from their colorful Mexico City apartment, featured here.

"From the beginning, we saw that there was an opportunity with this apartment to work with the designers that we were going to work with at the gallery. It gives us a great deal of pleasure to live with pieces that were made for us, and we connect with those pieces because it's part of this bigger arc of our lives."

"We started our gallery, AGO Projects, to work with contemporary designers, and to be working for the advancement of new things. Yet both of us also really love old things—we were so lucky that Rudy's grandparents had this incredible set of Soriana sofas [previous spread]—so there's this moment where the two collide for us. Our vision of the future is not slick. We're drawn to the idea that new things can also be cozy, and that new things can feel contemporary in spirit but still have traces of real handicraft or artisanal techniques, whether it's Fabien Cappello's chairs or the beautiful rug in the living room we commissioned from Agnes Studio."

"We love minimalism. It's totally extraordinary and wonderful to see. But none of our houses have been minimalist, even when the architecture has been very clean. Our houses are just vessels for objects and things."

“ The willingness to be inconvenienced or for something to be imperfect is a big part of our shared aesthetic—not over-art-directing or over-designing something until it no longer has any quirks or soul left. We both are drawn to stuff that feels experimental, that's not necessarily at its final stage.”

“ People have hierarchies around objects, design, and art, but we don't. Obviously, some things are more 'valuable' in terms of the market or in a context outside of our apartment. But we don't feel like artwork is devalued by having something in front of it that might not speak to it. We don't want to live in a gallery. In our home, it's all equally beautiful and it can all kind of jumble together.”

"The combination of materials in these chairs by Fabien Cappello—with the metal framework, the natural palm fiber, and the pony-skin headrest—is so strange. Postmodern and Memphis-y in some way, yet also tropical. They're very clearly a part of Fabien's language, and we were like 'We need to have them,' irrespective of how they were going to look with anything else in the room. That's part of the philosophy that's happening here—it all works together, but it also doesn't matter much to us whether it's working together."

"The chicken in the kitchen is a vintage piece—Mexican Majolica, probably from Puebla—that we had seen at a friend's house and admired. She moved and gave it to us. It's probably from the '50s, and it's just a wonderful found object. The fruit lamp by Fabien Cappello was developed for a show at AGO, and there's also a bronze version. We're not necessarily driven by the 'importance' of objects. We're drawn to things that make our lives more fun and elevate the way we're living."

"The dining table, called Dinner for Eight, was a commission for the apartment by Lanza Atelier, who were the subject of our first show at AGO. Theirs was the first real body of work we commissioned. In their work, Lanza tend to add an element of surprise or discovery, almost like a puzzle. People are always surprised at how the backs of the chairs fit perfectly into the top of the table. The scale and proportion are carefully considered to have an economy of material yet total comfort. It mixes a seriousness of design with a lightness of spirit."

"We both have an underlying desire to be cozy, and the way that we often achieve that is by combining different textural elements. In the guest room, it's the Fernando Laposse screen with its soft loofah panels, the nubby texture of the Chiaozza sculpture, the vintage rug on the floor, the wicker headboard. All of these things, in our mind, should live together, but it's almost subconscious. There's very little of the planning that we do for clients in terms of creating interiors for ourselves. It's much more accumulative."

"We have this conversation a lot with people that we're advising around furniture: If something is coming into your life and you're panicked about using it, then it's not worth having. There's a kind of casualness to our understanding of and approach to stuff. Some of these are beautiful vintage things that show forty, fifty years of age—that's partly what makes them so beautiful. We have nieces, we have nephews, we have dogs, we have parties—all of it is there to be used and to be part of our life."

"The Gaetano Pesce chair was a collaboration with Raf Simons that was exhibited and sold at Design Miami/Basel during Rodman's last year as creative director at Design Miami. It's made from mostly antique, nineteenth-century American quilts, and a lot of quilt lovers would be horrified that they were cut up. But we love that they were given a different life. Rodman has been collecting quilts since he was kid, and we love Raf as a designer, we love Gaetano, so every time we see it, it makes us happy because it represents this moment when all of these pieces of paper were kind of folded on top of each other for us in an exciting way."

EMBRACING DISCOMFORT

When you're putting together a home, it's often understood that your higher goal ought to be beauty, comfort, and ease. But we're here to champion the notion of living with objects that are confusing, or even a bit unsettling, if it's in the name of a higher artistic idea. Maybe it's a chair that looks like it might collapse when sat upon, or an object in the shape of a faintly grotesque body part. (In case you haven't noticed, body parts abound in this book.) Maybe the object is just mysterious to you because you can't immediately discern its materiality or function. If something makes you slightly uncomfortable—you like it, but couldn't picture it in your living room—that's okay, because it's going to be that much more thought-provoking than something that's merely pretty. Consider this our official endorsement for inviting objects into your space that are enigmatic, or even a little bit ugly. Here, five designers explain what inspired their strangest creations.

Ellen Pong
designer, New York City

" In 2019, I came across a photo of a charcuterie board online, and at first, I couldn't even recognize what it was. It was so grotesque looking. The image was burned into my mind after that. It was strange to think that someone had designed it to look that way. At the same time, I'd been thinking about all of the superfluous things that make up a home, like tissue-box covers, and somehow it made sense to me to turn that charcuterie board image into a tissue-box cover made of clay. I sometimes think about my practice as a kind of exorcism, where I'll be cursed with an extremely dumb idea for an object, and I have to make it in order to get it out of my mind.

People responded to it with a mix of interest and disgust, kind of like a car crash that you can't look away from. Maybe that's what's so appealing about it. But I'm not sure how it fits into a domestic space. I just see it as a little Trojan horse that I'm tossing out into the world. That's what I like about making furniture and home goods—they're easily consumable, and they let me insert my ideas into unexpected places."

Jonathan Muecke

furniture designer, Minneapolis

66 I was a student at Cranbrook when I made the Scrambler, in 2009. I'd recently gone to a Design Academy Eindhoven masterclass, and the instructors were talking about objects with narratives. I remember thinking, it *can't* just be that. It's not good enough for me. A narrative always limits you. You only get to tell one story. Whereas if the object is an exercise, there are different inputs and different ways of measuring them. I approached the Scrambler as an exercise in repeating something until enough of it was there. It had to be a certain size, and then it was complete. I drew lines on paper, like a diagram, until I could find a structure that was repetitive and self-stable. The piece is doing quite ambitious things structurally, continuously cantilevering over itself.

A lot of people at Cranbrook at the time were making things that solved their own problems. I need a bookshelf, I need a chair, or I bet someone else does. And I wasn't thinking that way. I still don't. I refer to my objects as relational objects—they change the objects around them as much as they represent themselves. That may be an imprint of my having been educated architecturally, where you talk about space and relationships to space. The Scrambler is easy to understand when you see the space within it next to the space outside it. In fact, someone else at Cranbrook gave it the name Scrambler, as a description of what it was doing. As an action object. (My name would have been something objective, like 'Tangential Wooden Shape.')

It's maybe not comfortable, but it's also not uncomfortable. In a way, my objects are ambivalent—they don't take up either of those positions. It's not about being disruptive, either. I generally regard the things I make as being quite generous and friendly, in fact."

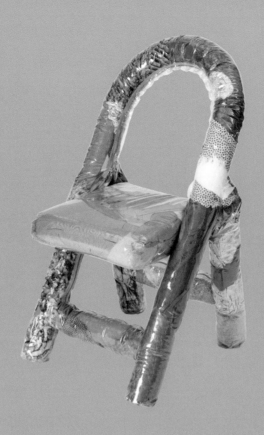

Katie Stout

furniture designer, New York City

We had to make chair models in one of my RISD furniture classes, and I had an old sweater I'd been carrying around that was too small. Whenever I wore it, I looked like a chubby toddler. I decided to knit it into a tiny stuffed chair. I liked the idea of a chair that looked like it had sort of given up, and I was really into the idea of a soft chair that you couldn't sit on—or at least looked like you couldn't sit on it.

After that, I decided to make these full-scale Stuffed Chairs, and the first ones were for the artist Bjarne Melgaard, as part of his installation at Karma Gallery in New York. I wanted the frame to have this caricature of a back—just a swoop, a clean line—so I looked at every single chair on the Internet until I found a metal folding chair from Home Depot that had the perfect silhouette, if I just removed the backrest. I made a vinyl slipcover for it, then stuffed it with printed fabrics, curtains, and personal objects as well, like Bjarne's old bank statements. I was relieved that they were received well, and surprised that any of them sold. They look like they're going to collapse. People were hesitant, like 'Can I sit on this?' You also think the back is going to be terrible, but it's actually comfortable. Though I don't know if people think it's more comfortable than it is because their expectations are so low.

I still make the chairs, and I fill them with scraps and off-cuts, because I never throw anything out. Sometimes I'll offer to include something personal from whomever is buying the chair, but also nothing's stopping anyone from putting their own stuff into it. It has a zipper. It's basically like one of those glass lamp bases that you can fill with Swedish Fish."

Sang Hoon Kim

furniture designer, Seoul

"I discovered flexible polyurethane foam in my childhood. My family has been operating a foam factory for three generations, so working with the material came naturally to me. But when I started helping the factory develop a new mattress line in 2015, that's when I began experimenting in earnest. I started learning about the characteristics of foam, and along the way, I discovered the possibility of using it to make unique furniture. I spent three years researching flexible foam, and my Foam Series is the result of that research.

Flexible foam is widely used in artificial skin, artificial leather, medical goods, mattresses, and pillows. It's harmless to humans and has no smell. It's a very suitable material for furniture because it's so comfortable. But my foam furniture is made very differently than other furniture. I don't need to do any drilling or cutting, and I don't need to add a finish, like lacquer, paint, or coatings. The foam itself has a built-in skin. To make it, I just use an electronic scale and a mixer to create various chemical formulations. By controlling the chemical reactions, I can control the properties of the foam, so that some parts of the piece might be soft, like a cushion, while others are hard enough to provide structural support. Then I create the design as if I'm modeling clay or drawing pictures. The process is very free and intuitive.

I choose the colors of each piece very freely, too, improvising my favorite colors each day according to my mood. So, this sofa, for example, changed color every day that I worked on it, as I added layers of foam. Once the colors felt like they matched, that's when it felt finished."

Tijmen Smeulders
product designer, Rotterdam

"In 2013, as a student at the Design Academy Eindhoven, I worked with a producer called Carpetsign, and that's where I first saw the polyester yarn that I used for my Parts Bench. It stood out because it had an interesting duality, being glossy along its length while on the ends, you got a beautiful absorption of light and color. It really stuck with me.

A few years later, I was developing a project with CNC tufting for an exhibition, and I came back to the polyester. At the time, I was very interested in the surface of a product—sometimes even more so than the functionality of it. In this case, the properties of the material dictated the bench's shape. I was focused on the dividing line on top and how the yarns fell down each side and created this lively surface. The form to me is passive; it's only the surface that has movement. It's constantly changing.

I think people were like, 'What is it? Is it an object or an abstraction?' And a lot of them reacted to it as being some kind of creature. That was funny to me because I was thinking, *Let's not talk about animals, let's talk about materials, and how it's made.* There's a lot of logic and thinking that went into the piece—why the yarns fall like that, how they meet the floor—and for me that took away the strangeness. How people reacted to it, as if it were a creature, was the only strange thing for me. I think the mystery was more interesting. When you question what you're looking at, and you can't grasp everything you see, something stays unclear. And then it's nice when, by using or exploring the object, you can discover much more."

162

Bottle with Stem and Slant by Robbie Frankel, 2021

THE HAND–
MADE
OBJECT

163

It can be hard to recall—in our post-industrial, nearly post-digital world—that once upon a time, everything in your home, on your body, and in the world was made by hand (and in some parts of the world, still is). If you needed something to wear, you sewed it yourself or had a dressmaker come to your house with a book of patterns. If you needed a place to eat, a carpenter would saw and sand your dining table. Ever wonder why historic homes smell so good? Engineered wood and Sheetrock may do nothing for the nose, but old-growth timber can retain its scent for years.

These days, in most industrialized economies, we have the ability to make nearly every object by machine. But handmade alternatives persist, cycling in and out of fashion, usually coming back into vogue either as a rebellion against our overreliance on technology or, in the case of DIY culture, in response to political upheaval or economic hardship. That's in part because there's something primally appealing about an object that's been made by a body at work. While machines can make objects more perfect and identical, hands can infuse each one with a soul. We've talked a lot in this book about how objects ought to appeal to your gut instinct, but handmade objects are the ones with the most potential to engage all of your senses. They often have lumps or bumps that you can run your fingers over—small imperfections in their form or finish that allow you to see evidence of the hand of the maker as they built or shaped the piece. And yes, some even emit the smell of something taken straight from the earth. As Catherine Lock of The New Craftsmen puts it, "I'm quite a believer in there being a portal or energy around handmade pieces. The basket in my entryway, for instance, still smells of sweet rush every time I step outside. There are layers of sensualness that come with craft that can really infuse an atmosphere."

Zesty Meyers, cofounder of the New York design gallery R & Company, goes even further: He believes we have something of a biological imperative that compels us to make, acquire, and live with tactile things. "I think it starts with our chemical makeup," he says. "There's something about holding a texture—whether it's cool or hot or rough or smooth—that we're inherently drawn to."

It may seem counterintuitive, but these quirks and imperfections actually give handmade objects more value and meaning rather than taking it away. They're not only the marker of something being one-of-a-kind, but they also help you understand how the object was made. What's more, they can lend objects a greater sense of authenticity. "We express ourselves through purchasing in this society," says Andrew Blauvelt, director of the Cranbrook Art Museum. "When everyone has the same light, everyone has the same chair, and we all shop at the same stores, the handcrafted object becomes a way for people to express their uniqueness. To give somebody a handcrafted item is considered intrinsically more meaningful than 'I found you the best thing at the store.'"

When incorporated into your home, handmade objects can add a bit of deliberate weirdness or intrigue to a space, often working to balance out the rectilinear perfection of a newly constructed apartment or the sheen of mass-produced goods. Jill, for instance, was recently on the hunt for a styling piece for her supersleek brass and laminate credenza; picking a squiggly-armed Morgan Peck vase—with its asymmetrical curves and wet-Barbie, eraser-pink glaze—turned out to be the perfect complement.

We'll be exploring several different types of handmade objects in this chapter. In the contemporary era, one of the more interesting trends has been the return to prominence of studio objects—i.e., pieces made by an artisan who's skilled in the use of a single material—only this time with a more experimental spin. Vintage handmade objects, if they aren't perfect already, can often be rehabbed or refinished into something even better. And then there are the objects you make with your own hands, which, depending on your patience for YouTube tutorials, may be more within your reach than you ever might have guessed. But before we delve into the forms that handmade objects can take, we thought it might be helpful to offer an overview of the context in which they've always been created.

A brief history

When people talk about the history of handmade objects, they're usually talking about the history of craft, which has long traditions that vary from civilization to civilization and are intimately tied to the cultures that cultivated them—like Mesopotamian flax weavers, Egyptian metalsmiths, Greek ceramicists, Korean lacquer artists, Ghanaian beaders, and American Shaker woodworkers. The earliest craft traditions arose primarily out of necessity, developed by populations that focused on whatever raw materials were available and then tailored them to suit their specific needs and aesthetics. They created huge knowledge bases around materials and

opposite: Tubes 21.12c Chair by Zaven, 2021
left: Vase by Attua Aparicio for SEEDS Gallery, 2019

techniques that, as trade grew and the world became a little more interconnected, could be tapped into and developed by artisans in other places as well.

Some of these handicraft traditions ultimately became so ubiquitous and co-opted that they're now taught in schools or workshops everywhere—we're constantly seeing young makers on Instagram trying their hand at raku, the sixteenth-century Japanese ceramic-firing technique, for instance—while others are, hundreds of years later, still entirely endemic to the specific places and communities that originated them. This is why it's extra important to ensure that if you're buying a handmade object designed by a Westerner and made by an indigenous artisan, the item honors and benefits the artisan rather than exploits or appropriates their techniques or culture.

Among non-indigenous cultures, the story of handmade objects in modern times is often linked to the perceived evils of mass-production. In the late 1800s, this took the form of the Arts & Crafts movement, which arose in reaction to the Industrial Revolution. As machines began to replace trained artisans, makers rose up to criticize the low-quality goods produced by mechanization and to assert the supremacy of handwork. The 1950s saw a similar surge in mass-production, but this time, progressive Western designers, like the Eameses and their Scandinavian peers, embraced it as the white knight that would finally enable them to make beautiful furniture inexpensive enough for everyone to own—a beacon of a more egalitarian society. In some ways they were correct, as "designed" furniture ultimately did go from something laboriously made in workshops for the ultrawealthy to something also sold at Ikea for $40. But that vision clouded in the subsequent decades, as it turned out that the tradeoff was often poor-quality goods, poor treatment of workers, or both—not to mention a sea of sameness. Those drawbacks ushered in the current era of veneration for the artisanal and the handmade, which by virtue of being constructed with care by an actual person, tend to be higher quality and more special than something spit out of a factory.

The rise of studio objects

As we mentioned earlier in this chapter, a renewed appreciation for handmade objects seems to recur cyclically in the design world, with renaissances occurring in the '70s, the '90s, and now today. The most recent rise is of course linked to a rejection of our digital and screen-based culture. In the same way that vinyl in recent years has come roaring back to the forefront among music enthusiasts, the most in-demand designers right now are those who channel a kind of analog warmth through their objects. Think of Katie Stout or Sean Gerstley's lamps and tables, with the thumbprint aesthetic of pinch pots blown up to life size, or Casey Johnson's wooden mobiles, whose lumpy silhouettes could be formed only by the designer sanding and shaping them by hand. The current design zeitgeist also owes a debt to design being impossibly, almost annoyingly, sleek in the early part of this century. (We

hope, like us, you've banished the memory of carbon-fiber furniture.)

But the current wave of practitioners also arose out of necessity. In the wake of the 2008 financial crisis, many designers were left figuring out how they could make things in their own studios, with limited teams and limited means, rather than having to pay expensive third-party fabricators. What resulted was a whole-hearted embrace of the kind of age-old, lo-fi techniques used to work with elemental craft materials such as glass, clay, metal, wood, and fiber. This is what set the stage for the resurgence of studio craft, a tradition that dates back to the nineteenth century but is most often associated with the 1960s, when artists like Peter Voulkos and Dale Chihuly were rethinking what it meant to work in ceramics and glass.

The new movement started in earnest around 2013, with the rise of statement ceramics made by an ever-growing roster of twenty- and thirty-something, mostly Brooklyn-based practitioners such as Helen Levi, Natalie Herrera of High Gloss, Forrest Lewinger of Workaday Handmade, Natalie Weinberger, and Isaac Nichols of Group Partner (the artist responsible for the once-ubiquitous, Instagram-famous "boob pot"). As a popular *New York* magazine article put it at the time, "As recently as a few years ago, New Yorkers who made pottery were considered a very specific type of latter-day hippie, congregating at studios like the century-old Greenwich House Pottery and hawking their bowls at craft fairs. But with the dawn of Etsy, Instagram, and the Brooklyn Flea, a new generation of pattern-playing, texture-bending ceramicists have emerged." Sight Unseen debuted our first ceramics pop-up in 2014, and what followed was a dizzying explosion of makers experimenting with clay, from Eny Lee Parker creating table bases in terracotta, to BZIPPY and Simone Bodmer-Turner vases becoming de rigueur Instagram décor, to Maxine Midtbo of Memor embedding shards of glass, seashells, and more into her viral ceramic vessels. On the more mainstream side of things, The Mug by East Fork Pottery got its own cult following and hashtag, like some sort of Alison Roman recipe. Seth Rogen became a potter.

A few years ago, we saw a similar revival in the world of handblown glass. At first, it was former glassmakers-for-hire, like Robbie Frankel of BaleFire or Andrew O. Hughes, who started to design and execute their own functional or creative ideas. Hughes took a break from churning out Calvin Klein glassware to make candlesticks inspired by California Light and Space artists; Frankel became known for speckled vases and

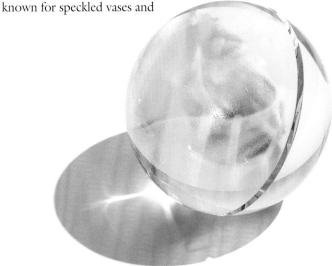

above left: Rock Vase I by Aleisha
Ellis, 2019

above right: Nose Vase by Oliver
Selim-Boualam and Lukas Marstaller
(BNAG), 2017

right: Velvet Artichoke by Rachel
Thomas for M.A.H Gallery, 2021

opposite: Mirror by Erika Kristofersson
Bredberg for The Ode To, 2020

cups that put an of-the-moment spin on Murano glass. Other seasoned glass artists like Anthony Bianco, John Hogan, and Thaddeus Wolfe made names for themselves in the world of high design. Soon, designers of all stripes—including Julie Richoz, Elyse Graham, Jonah Takagi, and Doug Johnston—were itching to experiment with glass, and pursuing residencies so they could collaborate with and work alongside glassblowers. As the trend grew, Sophie Lou Jacobsen's Ripple cups and Wave pitchers became household staples, Jochen Holz's artistic vessels were picked up by Hay while his more one-of-a-kind pieces became serious gallery fodder, and Danish designer Helle Mardahl took over the luxury circuit with her $600 candy-colored cache jars. Our thirst for all things glass also reanimated an obsession with formerly forgotten vintage specimens, from the ubiquitous Murano mushroom lamps to Kaj Franck goblets to Carlo Scarpa vessels, which were selling for six figures at Wright. Suddenly hand-blown glass, like handmade ceramics before it, had become a permanent signifier of style in our homes.

The new luxury

Though we've seen this same cycle play out in many different mediums, ceramics and glass remain eternal favorites. Both being incredibly temperamental mediums, there's such a high failure rate that it can sometimes feel like a tiny miracle when anything survives. Call it object mortality—sometimes it seems not a matter of *if* a piece will crack or break, but *when*. In

some ways, that's what makes these materials so appealing for makers to work with. Their very existence feels earned.

That note of uncertainty—along with the sheer amount of sweat equity that goes into their making, and the fact that each one is always a little different from the other—is also what makes handmade objects such cherished additions to a home. "In this day and age, when you can get anything at any time, the handmade is suddenly a scarcity," says Helena Carlberg, co-owner of the Swedish online objects destination The Ode To. "That's the new luxury—to find things that are special and have thought behind them." Carlberg is in a unique position to understand how handmade objects affect their owners, both on a visceral level and as part of a décor scheme: With her partner, Anna Lukin, she's turned even design students into aspiring collectors. Part of the appeal of handmade objects, she points out, is that their one-of-a-kind nature affords their makers more leeway for experimentation, color, and fun. Without the pressure of factory minimums, they have to worry about convincing only one person, not three hundred, to buy a particularly weird piece. "It's a special type of person who will put a piece of ceramic bacon on their wall," Carlberg jokes.

In that way, handmade objects often serve a similar function to art in the home—as talismanic chameleons that stay with you even as your tastes and apartments change. "When we move, sometimes we need different furniture," explains Carlberg. "But art stays with you, because even if your taste changes, it reminds you of who you were at that point in time."

above: Untitled vessels by Julien Carretero for A1043 editions, 2021

right: Bacon by Karol Zarbock for The Ode To, 2019

BUYING

Buying a handmade object isn't all that different from buying a piece of contemporary design. But as an aspiring collector, it helps to understand the craft techniques that make these particular pieces special. We've spent twenty years cultivating knowledge around how people make things, but to give you a crash course, we asked three designers working with three different materials to explain the processes behind their best-known series. Each of these designers started with an age-old technique and, by trial and error, turned it on its head to achieve pieces that are unlike anything we've seen before, and unlike anything their peers are making. Our hope is that these anecdotes not only fill you with the kind of buzzy excitement that we often feel when interviewing designers who are passionate about their work, but also help to inform your buying practices going forward—it's always magical to imagine the person behind the process.

CODY HOYT'S TESSELLATED CERAMICS

" I studied fine art and printmaking, so at first, clay was this fun, no-pressure thing—a diversion from my studio practice at that time. But once I get excited about something, I usually want to find ways to make it more complicated. The first wave of ceramic pieces that I made were planters, and one of the first things I wanted to do with them was to use two different colors of clay. With two colors, you can create a pattern on the surface that also becomes integral to the walls of the vessel. I had seen similar things at the Met—boxes with bone inlay or marquetry—and I'd also been looking at *nerikomi*, which is basically the Japanese version of what I wanted to do.

I started by mixing different colors of mason stain into white clay. Mason stain is a pigment that's designed to withstand the temperatures of an extremely hot kiln. The colors don't evaporate or burn out when the clay's being fired; they become more saturated. There are limitations on what colors you can make because the ingredients are natural, like cobalt or zirconium, but within a limited palette you can get a lot of variation.

To combine the colors, I used a marbling technique, which was super exciting because when you squish together a couple colors of clay, then slice through it and get that cross-section reveal, there's this thrilling aspect of, 'Whoa, that looks like stone.' Even though it's obviously not. I would marble together any number of colors, usually two or three, and extrude the clay into a shape. An extruder is basically like a pasta maker, where you push the clay through a pipe fitted with a die—a metal plate with a hole in it—and the shape of your die determines the shape of your 'noodle.' Then I'll slice the noodle. If it's in the shape of a diamond, for example, I'll get flat diamond tiles that I'll use to arrange the vase's external pattern, like puzzle pieces, on top of a slab of plain clay that prevents the tiles from detaching from each other when fired.

The majority of vessels that I make are geometric with hard edges. I start with the clay slab flattened out on the table, then stack it on top of an identical Sheetrock shape, then fold the whole thing up and tape it. At that point, I have a Sheetrock shell with a soft, wet, clay slab hugging the interior—basically a single-use mold. It stays that way for a few days, or sometimes weeks, until the clay dries out and is stable enough to live on its own.

In the last year and a half, I've started using the arrangement of the marbled inlays to create more representational scenes, like a landscape or a bouquet or a sunset. I came up with this technique of pushing colors of clay together and then dragging an edged tool across the surface in different ways to scoop off material. The chunk of clay that ends up coming off has a really interesting quality to it thanks to how the clay moved during the scoop. It's often very organic looking, and can resemble natural forms like leaves or petals.

I look at other designers, where there's a more direct line between their ideas and the finished objects, and I get frustrated that my process is so protracted. Sometimes ceramics feels like the wrong medium because it can take so long to see an idea through. I think I compensate for this lack of immediacy and spontaneity by focusing on the process itself and getting satisfaction from the experience. Hopefully the soul of it all resonates within the finished piece."

THADDEUS WOLFE'S ASSEMBLAGE GLASS VESSELS

" In art school, I was planning to study painting, but I got more excited by the process of blowing glass than I'd expected. I did a glass residency, and when I was there, I was making pieces based on mineral forms that I'd seen—hard-edged crystalline structures—where I'd blow the glass, and then grind and polish it. But I soon figured out that the only way to get the edges and textures I was going for was to make mold-blown pieces using a casting process. This method of mold making already existed, of course; basically it's a heated-up plaster and silica 'waste mold.' It's called that because you blow into the mold once and then destroy it in the process of removing it from the glass object.

I start everything by sculpting an object in Styrofoam. Sometimes I'll have a table full of foam scraps, and I'll put some of them together in a very improvised way, and other times, I'll have some concept of what the form is going to be and build it from there. I cut the Styrofoam into pieces and carve into it using X-Acto knives, wood saws, or utility knives, then I hot glue the pieces together. Once the form is basically finished, I encase it within a plaster and silica mix that takes on the texture of the model. I pour layers of plaster silica over the Styrofoam until it builds up to a couple inches in thickness, and then I remove the Styrofoam by hand using picks, clay tools, and a vacuum cleaner, leaving a hollow cavity to blow glass into.

I think what sets my work apart is how specific my forms are, and the way I'm experimenting with and using color. At the place where I blow glass in Brooklyn, they have two furnaces—one that's for clear molten glass, and then a small furnace that sometimes will have a color in it. But I would say for 90 percent of the pieces I've made, I haven't had the benefit of having that color already in the furnace. So, I

above: Untitled vessel by Thaddeus Wolfe for Volume Gallery, 2016

left: Untitled vessel by Thaddeus Wolfe for Pierre Marie Giraud, 2018

buy colors that come in the form of glass rods from Germany and from another company in New Zealand. Before blowing, I chop off a chunk of color and I melt that into what I call a color cup—basically a round-bottomed vessel that's blown freehand to size and color, depending on the piece they're intended for, that I can then fill with clear glass to create an interior layer.

When the glass is still hot and malleable on the end of the blow pipe, but it hasn't been blown yet into the mold, I can also roll it in powdered glass or melt glass shards on a metal table, or I can splotch on a few blobs of color. When the color rods are heated up, they're so soft you can kind of draw with a little chunk of colored glass on the outside of the vessel, like pulled taffy. The color incorporates once you've blown the piece in the mold. It's super low-tech, and there are a lot of things that can go wrong in the process, rendering the piece unusable—sometimes the piece can crack due to incompatible color combinations, and it's also difficult to judge how long to let the glass solidify after blowing into the mold. Too short and the piece will sag; too long and the piece will develop stress fractures. I've been doing versions of this for a while, though, and when they come out, they're not always perfect, but they're always different."

STEVEN HAULENBEEK'S ICE-CAST BRONZES

" In 2010, we got nailed with the most brutal winter Chicago has ever had. I was working with a metal foundry, and though I'd done some cast-bronze work before, I was able to really dig in. One day, I went outside and poured the hot casting wax into a little crack in the sidewalk that had frozen over with ice. It looked like shit, like a cow patty. But there was just enough information that I could see a temperature shock from the hot wax seizing as it hit the cold ice, creating a rippled texture that looked like growth patterns—nature's geometry. I started to put things in my kitchen freezer, like metal bowls or other objects, and I would pour hot wax into them to see what happened.

Lost-wax casting is a centuries-old process, and normally it starts by carving or forming an object in clay or some other material. You create a mold around that object, and use it to produce a positive replica of the sculpture in wax. You dip the wax model into a ceramic slurry and then into a powder of silica sand, over and over until there's a thick shell coating it. Then, you put the entire thing into the kiln, which melts the wax and provides a hollow space into which you can pour the bronze. The bronze ends up with the same shape and texture as the wax model. In my process, I'm using carved ice as a way to create an original pattern directly in wax, as opposed to starting in clay. You would think that ice is just ice, but pouring into minus-10-degree ice is totally different than pouring into 20-degree ice. Warmer ice or cooler wax will create a wider ripple, and colder ice or hotter wax will produce these tiny micro ripples. I've found the sweet spot within that,

but it's always interesting when you pop the wax out. You never know what it's going to look like.

Eventually, I started to scale up. First, I bought big, wholesale blocks of ice. Then, I bought an ice-cream freezer off Craigslist and started freezing my own blocks. I also started to do work on location, where I'd travel to a frozen lake and pour wax there, or I'd go onto the flat rooftop outside my studio window, put a sprinkler out there, and ice it over like a skating rink. Sometimes, I'd fill up a kiddie pool or a Rubbermaid trash can bit by bit and allow it to freeze over. Then, I'd carve out the interior using a die grinder with rasp bits, or hand tools, like chisels. Another time, I packed a big snowball in my backyard—four feet in diameter—and carved out the interior, then hosed it down for a couple of days until it was icy enough to cast wax in.

My neighbors think I'm a weirdo, but working outdoors has allowed me to work at a different scale and with a more free-form production technique, using ephemeral conditions to create permanent objects. It becomes a timestamp of where and when and how these objects were made. I've always gravitated toward experimenting with materials, where the aesthetic was not entirely determined by me, and what I love about the ice-cast bronze is that it feels like a collaborative process between myself and nature. I create the framework by which the process can occur, but the details are created by something beyond me. I could never design these pieces the way that they look, and I think they're special for exactly that reason."

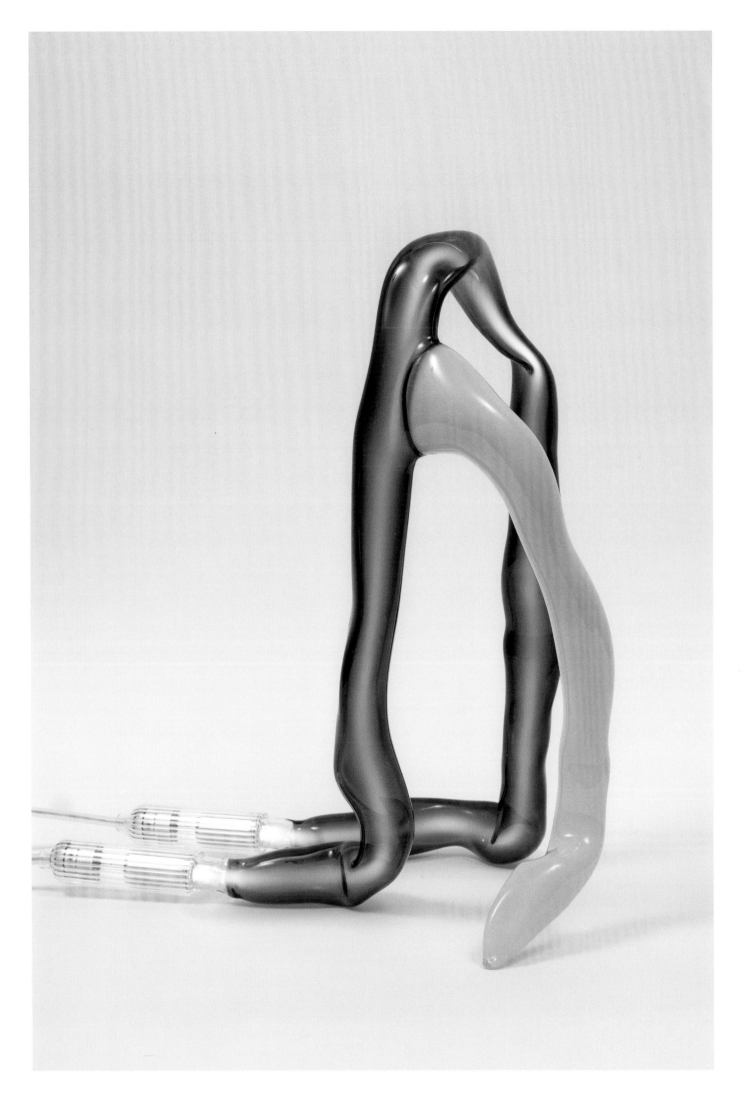

opposite: Sculptural neon light by Jochen Holz for The Future Perfect, 2021

above left: Unique piece in handblown glass by Boris de Beijer, 2021

above right: Tasmania Vase by Elyse Graham, 2017

left: Wiggle Vase in Cinnamon by BZIPPY, 2018

MAKING

In 1974, the late Italian designer Enzo Mari published *Autoprogettazione?*, a DIY instruction manual that taught readers how to build nineteen rudimentary furniture projects using only wooden slats, a hammer, and some nails. The book was free (a rarity in the pre-Internet world), and Mari hoped that the projects would help people understand how good design works, and that it transcends materials and price tags. It wasn't the first book to address these ideas—DIY manuals go all the way back to the 1600s, when a volume called *Mechanick Exercises* advised readers on things like blacksmithing techniques and cartography—but in the design world, it's probably the most enduring and influential. Mari not only presaged the open-source and MakerBot movements by decades, but he also inadvertently provided a kind of aspirational blueprint for a DIY spirit that continues to this day.

It's important to note that DIY projects are not always motivated by saving money, or even by the kind of type-A perfectionism that compels people to do things to their own exacting standards. Like other modes of self-production that have flourished in recent years, from baking bread to tie-dying, making an object with your own hands can be both a therapeutic pursuit and one that telegraphs something about who you are to the outside world. Just before quarantine, *New York* magazine published an article exploring the skyrocketing number of nonexperts who had taken to building Donald Judd furniture from scratch. Having a piece of home-cooked Judd furniture in your apartment, writer Hilary Reid explained, might signal to visitors that you possess both a higher level of design savvy and "a level of technical skill beyond that required to assemble an Ikea Billy Bookcase. It's the rare project that simultaneously lets you flex a knowledge of art history and (some) capacity for manual labor."

At a time when so much of modern life can seem like an exercise in futility, taking on a home improvement project—where both the endpoint and the steps to getting there are clearly delineated, often on YouTube—can generate a real sense of purpose. It's also a way to foster the kind of memorable narrative we've been talking about, one that lends a sense of meaning to your surroundings. Which will you remember more, hiring a contractor to construct a brick hearth or laying your own using colorful tile remnants, the way designer Ellen Van Dusen did when she renovated the nonworking fireplace in her Brooklyn brownstone? "It's nice to feel connected to your home in that way," says Van Dusen. "Everything I did myself in my house, I feel even more proud

of. Learning these processes, even if you don't master them, is fun. And for me, it also helps me think about my own work in a new way." Blauvelt agrees: "It's generative and empowering for people to be able to make something," he says. "The country tends to go through phases. The GIs came back from World War II and there was a big home improvement thing going on, then my generation never learned how to do anything except call repair people. Now I think it's a form of stress release for a younger generation."

Elise McMahon, the Hudson Valley–based designer known for her inventive reuse of discarded materials, from blue jeans to brake rotors, connects the embrace of DIY to both the personal and the political. "You're basically wanting to remove yourself from the normal consumer model that the American capitalist system wants you in," she says. "But in the last decade, there's also been such a strong interest in materials and the transparency of processes that I think it inspired a lot of people to not be afraid to just try." Some of her favorite DIY books are from the 1970s, generally considered the golden age of DIY manuals; they range from philosophical narratives that

12/00 Mug by Lalese Stamps, 2019

explore the DIY ethos, to more instructional classics like Peter Stamberg's *Instant Furniture*, to James Hennessey and Victor Papanek's *Nomadic Furniture*, which "draws out DIY furniture projects from bunk beds to butterfly chairs," McMahon says. If you're looking for more inspiration, we also highly recommend tracking down *How to Construct Rietveld Furniture* by Peter Drijver or *Easy to Make Furniture* by the editors of *Sunset* magazine, which will instruct you in the art of fashioning avocado-hued cushioned seats on a PVC pipe frame, or beanbag-esque body pillows.

If you're looking for a more contemporary spin on DIY, there are certain books that fulfill that niche as well, including two great volumes called *DIY Furniture* and *DIY Furniture 2* by the contemporary designer Christopher Stuart. These will teach you how to make truly next-level pieces like a macramé hanging chair designed by Ladies & Gentlemen Studio, or a set of Split Box Shelves, originally conceived by British designer Peter Marigold.

For something a bit less intimidating, the Internet can once again be your friend. Serious online design tutorials can be hard to find, because most blogs and DIY TikToks skew more toward stenciled backsplashes and reclaimed wood bookshelves, à la HGTV queen Joanna Gaines. But *Domino* magazine's archives can be an excellent resource, especially when you want to hit the higher-end design trends—covering a thrifted cabinet with burl wood contact paper, making a vintage-inspired knife-pleated lampshade—and so can *Architectural Digest*'s "AD It Yourself" section. Instagram accounts to follow include @thishouse5000 in Toronto (cane headboards) and @flex.mami in Sydney, Australia (resin coasters, spray-foam mirrors). If you simply want in on the spirit of DIY but lack the power tools to get there, studios like the Los Angeles–based Loose Parts will send you a pre-prepared open-source kit of hardwood rails, metal panels, and steel fasteners to build shelves and garment racks with a kind of haute–Erector Set aesthetic.

above left: Untitled (Buttends) by Marco
Kane Braunschweiler for Marta Gallery, 2016

above right: Vase by Memor Studio, 2019

left: Chisel Mirror by Studio Anansi, 2018

opposite: Poly Rainbow 60 Chair by Max
Lamb for Salon 94 Design, 2020, courtesy of
the artist and Salon 94 Design, New York

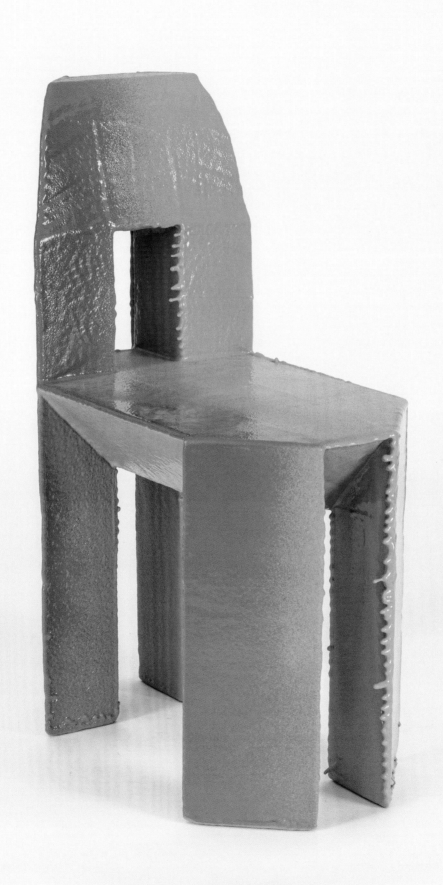

REHABBING

If the idea of building a piece of furniture from scratch is too much of a stretch, allow us to advocate instead for creative reinvention—from refinishing a nightstand to turning a sculpture into a lamp. Most people, when they come across an object that's not quite right, simply forget to ponder the possibilities for transformation before they pass it by. Others don't have the patience for dramatic rehab projects. But pretty much everyone who's able-bodied can wield a paintbrush and turn a plain white table Yves Klein blue, or take a cherry-red console back to classic white. It's the easiest possible makeover, and yet you have to train your mind to see that kind of potential.

"Paint is a very easy solution to make a great impact," says designer Keren Richter, cofounder of the New York interiors studio White Arrow, who has rehabbed countless objects in projects for both her clients and herself. "To do it right can be a laborious process that involves multiple steps with lots of attention to detail. But if you're looking for a weekend project, you can obviously just slap a coat of color on something and make it look nice." She told us a story about two Tobia Scarpa sofas she'd bought on LiveAuctioneers for her Brooklyn home: "They were totally beige, both the frame and the leather," she says. "But the look of our living room was more about cool tones with pops of saturated color, so I repainted the frames with white oil-based lacquer, then took the cushions to my shoe repair guy and had him color the leather white. Some would say that's sacrilegious, but I think it's better to keep using something with a beautiful silhouette that's made of real wood than to buy some MDF throwaway."

Paint is an obvious choice when fixing up vintage finds. But it can also be a less-obvious way to elevate an off-the-shelf everyday object. Years ago, when we visited the home of knitwear designer Annie Lee Larson for Sight Unseen, we remember falling in love with a terracotta planter—the kind you'd find at any hardware store—that she'd color-blocked in glossy blue, peach, yellow, and green. It was a simple intervention, but one that spoke volumes about Larson's aesthetic point of view. When we interviewed Van Dusen for this book, she told us about similar upgrades she'd made in her Brooklyn home: "When I was shopping for table lights, it was hard to find cute ones that were also affordable, so I decided to paint stripes on some that I'd bought in Chinatown. They had rectangular stainless-steel bases and two bulbs that looked like little pills. I got a metal primer in white, then painted over it with purple and green stripes on one, and pink and red on the other. In the end, they looked super cute, people always ask me about them, and they only cost $50."

Other upgrades can be easy to achieve on your own as well—like finding a new lampshade for a great base—but if you're thinking about a more elaborate rehab, such as refinishing a wood table or reupholstering a chair, it's important to assess whether a piece is worth investing in at all. As they say, it often comes down to good bones. "At the end of the day, it has to do with what it was originally made of," says Richter. "If a chair is made from fiberboard and staples, you're gonna have to remake the whole thing anyway, so what's the point?" Some questions to consider: If the piece is made from wood, is it solid wood or is it veneer, which can be hard to refinish? If there's an upholstered cushion, is the fill made from down-wrapped foam or horsehair (preferable), or polyester (not as desirable)? "I once found a 1940s Italian sofa at auction for fifty euros," says Richter. "It had horsehair fill, and it was amazingly constructed. The reason it was so cheap is that it was ripped and falling apart; most people would have said, 'What a piece of garbage.' But it had a great silhouette, and after I reupholstered it in a mustard Rose Uniacke fabric, it looked really chic and luxurious."

If you don't know how to answer those questions simply by looking at a piece (and don't worry, we wouldn't necessarily

Tiered side table by Joe Hartley for The New Craftsmen, 2021

either!), ask around. Obviously if you've purchased the piece online, you should ask the seller any questions you might have about its construction. But if you've purchased an object in a more anonymous way, such as by finding it on the street or inheriting it from a family member, start with a more design-savvy friend, a local vintage shop, or a neighborhood-focused network like Nextdoor, Facebook, or Angi. It also doesn't hurt to seek out even more specialized subgroups online; Facebook alone is home to thousands, like The Mid Century Modern Furniture Refinishing Resource. "We have a specific type of oven—an old AGA range—and there's a very active community just for that oven," says Richter.

If you really can't or don't want to rehab something yourself, you might opt to use those same resources to find a professional who can do it for you. Once you have some recommendations under your belt, start with something small, like a pillow or a chair, to test out the quality of that vendor's work. "It's hard for people outside the industry to understand what makes a good workroom, but for an upholsterer, for example, you want the seams to be straight and the fill to be of a good quality, you want to be able to sit-test it, and you want to make sure the communication is very clear—that if there's a problem, they'll tell you ahead of time," says Richter.

Like everything in life, rehabbing can involve trial and error, and pitfalls abound. (Take one look at the Instagram account @whydidyoupaintthat to see exactly what we mean.) But it can also be a great way to transform pieces you love and keep them in circulation rather than writing them off if they're damaged or otherwise superficially unlovable. "Once you realize the possibilities," says Richter, "you'll start to see the potential in anything."

Tile Block Table #4 by Sean Gerstley for Superhouse, 2020

182

At home with

KIM
MUPANGILAÏ

Born and raised in Belgium, **Mupangilaï** is a Belgian-Congolese interior architect, furniture designer, and graphic designer who lives with her boyfriend in a 1920s brownstone in Brooklyn. Its original period details offer the perfect backdrop for her extensive collection of vintage handmade objects, which she also sells through her side project, the online shop En la Mésá.

" For me, objects don't always need to have a meaning, but I do always admire pieces from different cultures. My partner and I both have our own heritage: I'm Belgian Congolese and he's Mexican American. So I always gravitate to pieces with a history. The funny thing is, we always thought it was important to bring both of our cultures into our home, but there are so many similarities between central Africa and Mexico when it comes to furniture and wood sculpting. Certain pieces could be from one place or the other."

"The little black bowl on top of this cabinet was made by Charlyn Reyes, a Canadian ceramicist. She has a strong connection to her Latin heritage in her work, which I love. The candlestick is from the '80s, by Anna Everlund. The mirror is contemporary, but I don't know the maker, and the candleholder is vintage."

"I look at material combinations, colors, textures, and heights when I put together vignettes, trying to create some sort of depth. I make sure everything matches or works visually. Basically, every surface in our house is available to put stuff on."

"I'm drawn to organic, imperfect objects rather than something perfectly shaped and angled. Objects with a narrative or a story that have lived, so to speak. That's why vintage pieces are so unique—you know they've been in another person's home or traveled from another country. Even if I don't necessarily know the story, I like knowing there's something behind it."

"This table was made by my friend who's a furniture designer, Thomas Serruys. The chairs are from the dealer Carmen Nash of Loft and Thought. The tall ceramic piece is by the New York ceramicist Danny Kaplan, and the bowl and cup on the mantel are hand-carved wood. Lately, though, I've been trying to break the style of the mantel with objects that are a little more Postmodern or colorful. I have turquoise ceramic candleholders on it now. The mantel is pretty wild if you think about how people made this all by hand—I can't even imagine how much time that must have taken."

"This fireplace blew my mind when I saw it. It almost looks like an Egyptian pyramid. I'm almost positive it was used for cooking back when the house was originally owned by one family. The tall white vessel is from Simone Bodmer-Turner, who I used to work with, and the head I found at a Brooklyn plant store. Both chairs are vintage. The wood one I found outside of a hotel; they were throwing it out."

66 My dad migrated from the Congo to Europe in the late 1970s, and there were a couple of African-made pieces he took with him and never got rid of. When I grew up, he passed them on to me. He gave me the tall object that's on top of my living room credenza, among a couple of other pieces. It's really nice to have a piece of my heritage in my New York home. The little hammer-looking thing above was originally a two-part nutcracker, but I just loved the hammer on its own. I wouldn't even use it as a hammer; it's like a sculpture." ↑

190

At home with

LISA
MAYOCK
& JEFF
HALMOS

"The perforated leather sculpture in the corner of the living room was actually once a conveyor belt in a factory that sorted oranges. I bought it on Chairish. I just thought it was a beautiful object and a great color. A gigantic zipper runs all the way down the side; it's very industrial looking. I bought it originally to use it as a screen, but that was a DIY project that just never happened. But I like that it also functions as a kind of piece of Pop art."

Before moving to Los Angeles with their two children, **Mayock and Halmos** met in New York City, as designers of the cult-favorite fashion brands Vena Cava and Shipley & Halmos. After a brief stint co-running the graphic T-shirt line Monogram, they've both branched out into new lines of work—Mayock as an interior designer and Halmos in commercial real estate development.

" In a previous life, I had a fashion brand called Vena Cava, and I made this wall hanging from one of our archive textiles. We wanted more yellow in the living room, so I looped a couple of yards of fabric around a metal architect's ruler that's nailed into the wall. I just love how it goes with the blue Chinese Art Deco rug, and I love the scale of it—that you can really see everything from far away." ↓

" We found this colorful handmade sculpture in Florida, where Jeff is from. We often get lucky sourcing things there because the aesthetic is more from the '80s and '90s—it's more fun, and it has a sense of humor, which is very much our sensibility. We don't love anything that's too serious. There has to be something in a room that's funny or maybe kind of ugly, that subverts things that might otherwise be too pretty or coordinated." ↑

"Our house is a 1920s Spanish-style two-story, and when we moved in five years ago, the dining room felt very dark, with lots of different wood tones. I thought it would be great if we had a table with a light-colored top, but I couldn't find one, so I had the oval metal frame made by a friend who is a metal-worker, and I went to a discount tile warehouse deep in LA. I bought a bunch of different whites and smashed them with a hammer in my driveway. I set them into place, then grouted the whole thing. The entire process probably took two days and halfway through, I thought for sure I had completely ruined it because there was grout everywhere. But it turned out pretty well. It has a few stains from our kids and it's very irregular, but that's part of the charm." ←

"Almost everything in our house is either handmade or vintage. On the whole, I don't see a lot of new things that I'm drawn to, and I really like things that have a patina. It just looks more authentic. Often, I get things and tweak them just a bit. For example, with the dining room chairs, I found a set of four on eBay and then a set of two on Etsy. They were completely different colors and I was like, 'This would be so great if they were black,' so I reupholstered them in faux leather. I also really like using things that are meant for one purpose for a totally different purpose. We have a '70s ice bucket that, in our house, is used to hold Polaroids. Part of me sometimes wishes I could turn that part of my brain off, but I can't. I just think it is so fun to think of all the possible paths your space could take."

"I love collecting small silver pieces. They're like jewelry for your room. In the living room, there are three silver cubes with rounded caps. I think they're meant to store perfume or oils, but they're beautiful as sculptures. The silver lamp in the living room I found at a junk store and walked right past because it's mirrored on every surface. It was 100 percent camouflaged. And in the bedroom, on the black lacquered dresser, is a silver penis. It's like if Elsa Peretti made a dick sculpture. It's just the most beautiful, elegant rendering of it, and it's funny and beautiful at the same time. I feel like it really sums up the things that I love."

"I guess the person who made this wire sculpture had found a dumpster full of old cords in the back of a company that produced electronics. I don't know if they came in these colors or if they were able to recolor them, but they basically spooled the cords into cylindrical shapes and melted them together. I thought it was the most beautiful example of treasure trash. I love when you walk into a space and see something and you're like, 'I love that. I have no idea what it is.' The framed photo of the egg behind the sculptures is by Wary Meyers."

At home with
MINJAE
KIM

200

Born in Seoul, trained in New York as an architect, and now a full-time furniture designer, **Kim** creates sculptures in wood and fiberglass that reimagine Western design archetypes—like the chaise longue, the executive desk, or the prayer seat—through the lens of Korean craft techniques. His home in Queens is an extension of his research, filled with studio experiments and the remnants of his former life in South Korea.

" I have a huge interest in '80s or Postmodern standalone wardrobes, and as I was studying them, I realized there were a lot of examples that mimicked rural sheds. During the pandemic, I spent a lot of time in my backyard, and there was always a need for storage because my neighbor, who I share the yard with, does a lot of farming and gardening. At the same time, I wanted to make the backyard space a little bit more my own. When I had some extra time for a holiday break, I decided to go for it and built the shed."

"During the pandemic, my roommate was doing a lot of natural dyeing upstairs while I was working in my woodshop downstairs, and we had been talking about working together. I didn't want my work to take over the space. For the pendant above the kitchen table, she made a naturally dyed silk shade and I built a frame and wired it. We also built this fabric hanger in the living room together. She had all of these fabric samples piled up, and one day I was at the studio and I had an idea to make a kind of skeleton figure. It was another way to bring our work together in the space that we share."

" The paintings in my apartment are all by my mom, MyoungAe Lee. I grew up with her work. When I was in elementary school she was in grad school, so I spent a lot of time in that environment. When there started to be more opportunities to share my work here, I wanted to bring her in as well. Although I'd never had a chance to put my work next to hers physically, I always had a sense that there was a connection. Being able to create work or space that complements hers feels really rewarding to me." ←

" I try to not treat anything in my house too preciously; it's all a bit more ad hoc. And we've definitely had accidents because something's not quite bolted or fixed. But I like that type of impracticality, and I like the rituals that result from that impracticality in your living space. If everything worked perfectly, you would never think about it. But when everything's a little iffy, it makes you a little more aware. You start to develop little rituals of how you open a door or how you sit at a table. I find it very enjoyable, and home is really the only place I can do that."

"Rarely do I make a chair thinking that it's for myself. Usually it happens afterward. My fish chair, for example, was something where I wanted to get the idea out, but then I felt really connected to it, so I'm not planning on ever selling. At home, I don't have much pressure for things to be a certain way. I see it as a place where my work can flow through and people around me can enjoy it, make fun of it, all of that. Between the years that I spent abroad and being an immigrant, there was always that question of, 'What is my home identity?' Because it's not Korean, it's not American. So, I try to keep the pieces that are most personal to me, which is often work that I'm most hesitant to explain."

"Because I lived abroad for so long, it got to a point where I needed to reinvent the idea of home for myself. The best way for me to do that is to build things for myself. When I moved in, the bedroom had a swing door to the outside and no closet. It was so tight that I had to throw out my bed frame. I built a closet and a bookshelf and made it kind of an entry moment. Then I worked on the bed frame, which is made from second-grade plywood. After that, it was figuring out what gestures could accommodate my objects, like adding a knob to the bookshelf to hold a cup, and making a little desk. I had some satinwood and ebony bark that I'd gotten from a lumberyard sitting around, so those were used as accents to go with a kind of plywood box."

DESIGNER
DIYS

In the early days of Sight Unseen, we published a column called
Artist's Proof, named after the practice of artists keeping, for their
own archives, the first piece in a numbered edition. In our column, we
featured objects that designers had made for themselves, that they
had no intention of ever producing or selling. Sometimes these items
were the result of studio experiments that ultimately weren't fit to
commercialize, but usually they were created to fill a specific need in
the designer's own home, such as a display cabinet for a collection or a
sofa with a particular shape. For us, they were fascinating in that they
offered a more personal, private glimpse into the designer's practice,
capturing a rare moment when their creativity wasn't constrained by
the needs of a client or the market. Here are five of our favorite current
examples, along with anecdotes about what impulse inspired them,
how they were made, and why they've earned a cherished place among
the designer's possessions.

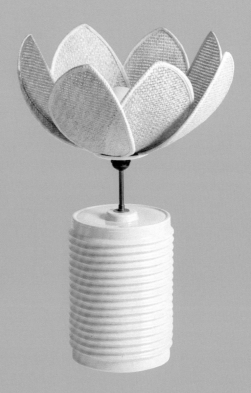

Clarisse Demory
designer and stylist, Paris

" I was helping my parents design their new guest room, and it needed a lamp. My first reflex is always to wonder if there's anything I can reuse so I don't have to buy something new. Besides the ecological considerations, embellishing and optimizing existing pieces to reveal their potential is one of my main sources of satisfaction in life. It really makes me happy.

My mother keeps, at her place, all the objects and furniture that I find in thrift stores. It helps me with future interiors and editorial projects, so I can amass a collection of beautiful things instead of searching for a needle in a haystack each time I need something. To make this lamp, I just put together things I'd saved: a vintage ceramic lamp stand, a vintage shade from a ceiling lamp, a large contemporary bulb. When I saw the shade, I realized it would create a flower shape if I turned it upside down. And so this useful object became very decorative, which is a nice moment in our minimalist room, with its cement floors. It also somehow modernized the feel of the shade's very typical '70s/'80s design and made me like it better.

My work is driven by the strong belief that we must work in a sustainable way and recycle as much as we can, but at the same time it has to be creative and elegant so it can apply to the most sophisticated fields. The challenge is, how can we recycle but make something contemporary and fresh at the same time? This is where creativity hides, and probably humankind's salvation, too: in our ability to create something new with the old, something beautiful with the disregarded."

Phoebe Sung & Peter Buer

designers, Cold Picnic, New York City

"During quarantine, we had to completely gut and redo our house in Queens because we found lead in the walls and our kid had high blood levels. We had a tenant upstairs who was leaving, so we decided to turn two units into one but keep the second kitchen. Both kitchens are really, really tiny; we needed to make a table and chairs to fit the upstairs one because we couldn't find anything small enough. We don't really know how to make furniture, so we just made this very petite set from the thick cardboard tubes that our custom rugs come with. We chopped them up and then papier-mâchéd layers and layers and layers. They're very heavy to pick up; scooting a chair out is kind of a job.

Both of us have always been impulsive, so we often make things because we can't find them as fast as we need them. We used to make dioramas to showcase our rugs for photo shoots, because we were like, 'We don't know anyone who has this room, so let's just make it.' When we first started Cold Picnic, we made everything that we sold by hand—jewelry, bags, soap, wall hangings. It got to the point where someone would place an order and it would ruin our day because we knew we couldn't do anything else for the next few days. It was exciting when we started to work with factories, because design was the fun part. It was a luxury to not be held back by what we could make ourselves. Of course, now that we've been outsourcing everything for so long, it creeps back in that you want to build something on your own. We've been making things around the house, and it's starting to take over."

Emmanuel Olunkwa
designer and editor-in-chief of PIN-UP, New York City

"I had a circular table in my apartment that used to sit against the wall, and it just didn't feel great. There's a formality to a circular table that prevents you from engaging with people, because everyone's floating in this weird way. I decided to make a plywood table with petals, a shape that evolved based on my desire to create intimacy. But before I even decided to make a table, I knew that each chair around it was going to be different. I felt like when you're in my home, I want you to sit down and be able to represent what you're feeling with where you're sitting. To be able to sit in your truth.

My last name starts with an O, and I've always loved circles. They're basically my version of the infinity sign. I made the Keyhole chair first, and then an arch is kind of a continuation of that infinity theory. There's also a square-backed version, which felt like a masculine-feminine, natural complement to the arch. A friend was visiting New York, and we were sitting in Washington Square Park, and she was like 'It's so cool how your chairs are imitations of various arches.' And I was like, 'What?' I didn't even realize I had been articulating those shapes. But it's true: The chairs for me are gateways. They're portals in a religious sense, but also in an architectural sense. They take you to another place."

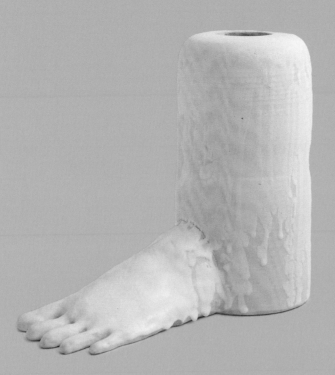

Forrest Lewinger
ceramicist, Workaday Handmade, New York City

66 For Workaday Handmade, I'm in the studio every day cranking out multiples of the same object. Sometimes I'll start looking around at them and imagining what they'd look like if they were changed or combined with other pieces. What if the bowls were stacked on top of each other? What if this handle was larger than you'd imagine a handle to be? When my work starts to feel too repetitive, making something for myself like that gives me a moment to react against what I normally do.

In this case, so much of my work in the past had been a combination of form with color or pattern. I hadn't really gone in a figural direction. One day I thought, 'What about a stool with some other object sticking out of it?' I think the foot was an attempt at visual humor. The pun 'footstool' was in the back of my mind, but I also chose a foot because it's such an odd body part. Eyes, noses, mouths—you see those all the time. The foot is generally something you hide.

The plan was to make a stool, but I started with a vase as a test for proportion. It works specifically because it's so weirdly proportioned—the foot is almost as long as the vase is tall, so it takes up just as much weight and emphasis. And it creates a nice juxtaposition between the more abstract and the more pictorial.

Workaday, for me, started out as an artistic proposition, and then it turned into a business. When I live with these objects that are a little outside of that, it brings me back into a more artistic mode. It reminds me that thinking about these larger, abstract ideas needs to be a part of what I do in the studio every day."

Pat Kim

designer, New York City

" My wife had been asking for a bed frame for a long time. I prefer a simple mattress situation, but I thought it would be a good opportunity to try to build something I never had before. Beds can actually be pretty simple to construct, so I was limited in the number of design choices I could make.

The headboard was the big thing; I went through 20 different iterations of sketching it and cutting out little models. I really liked the idea of the Ellsworth Kelly gingko-leaf shape, but my wife was like, 'You can do better than that.' So I just went for it, drawing on the actual piece of headboard wood and erasing it, and then drawing over it again—a lot of spontaneous experimentation, cutting things off, and gluing them back on. I cut and shaped it entirely by hand using saws, rasps, and other tools.

The bed is made from American black walnut. I'd glued up the wood with the grain running horizontally, and the squiggles go up and down, so it ended up a little floppy. If I were to design it again, I'd do the grain going the other way. But it's sturdier than I thought it would be. I made it as well as I could, because I want it to be something that I pass down.

I've probably built 90 percent of the furniture in our house. Even though this apartment is temporary, it's still a stepping-stone, so I've built benches, coffee tables, a kitchen island, cutting boards, Shaker rails with pegs for hanging stuff up. I love making things for the house, and I love living with them. It's a way for me to see when something's not practical, or when I want to change a proportion. I also feel more invested when I'm working on something knowing that I have to see it every day for possibly the rest of my life."

214

Ceramic sculpture, mid-century.

From the collection of LA interior designer Martha Mulholland, who acquired it from the estate sale of a woman she felt strongly connected to.

THE SENTI-
MENTAL
OBJECT

A few years ago, we came across an Instagram post by the Brooklyn ceramicist and florist Aviva Rowley, depicting a truly strange object on a table in her home: a storage box for nail polish whose "lid" was a foot-long, three-dimensional severed finger with a long, dark fingernail. "A gift from my father, who carved it from wood and gave it to me when I was 7," she wrote in the caption. "It's one of my most prized possessions." That post perfectly captures the power of sentimental objects—whether they're beautiful, and whether they're valuable, their indelible ties to a particular time, place, or person make us feel a particularly strong emotional attachment to them. They function as physical stand-ins for our memories, offering us a specific kind of comfort when we integrate them into our homes. When Rowley passes that box on her way out of the house each day, she doesn't just see a funny, witchy finger; she sees a sweet reminder of her dad.

　　Sentimental objects can be vintage or contemporary, designer or anonymous, manufactured or handmade, which means that many of them may fit equally as well into other categories discussed in this book. But because they're emotionally supercharged—and as such often live outside the realm of aesthetic considerations—we thought they merited their own discussion and celebration. In other words, a sentimental object is less likely to be one treasured *primarily* for its pedigree or its trendy formal expression: it may just be a beautiful rock given to you by your best friend, or a ceramic bowl you found at a craft market on the first trip you ever took with your romantic partner. Whatever you felt then for the person, place, or time of your life associated with that rock or bowl is what you'll feel again when you look at it now. We keep these objects not because they look good or make us look good, but because we find them moving.

"We get so caught up in whether objects have monetary or social value," explains the Mexico City art and design curator Su Wu, whose widely documented home is full of unusual artifacts whose meanings are known only to her. "Sentimental objects have a different kind of value." When we interviewed Fanny Singer of Permanent Collection, who with cofounder Mariah Nielson produces limited runs of housewares and clothing items based on the cherished possessions of their friends and loved ones, she attempted to define that value: "That extra question of sentiment—it's not just affection or love, it's something ineffable that almost makes it another category," she says. "I think it's being surrounded with reminders of your own story." And as Wu reminds us, "There's that saying that if you get to tell the story of your life, then you get to live your life twice." Sentimental objects transform our homes into a rich visual diary.

A primal connection

We all own objects like this, even those of us whose living rooms are filled with priceless collectibles as well. In fact, if Sight Unseen called you up tomorrow and asked to interview you about your own most truly prized possession—the one you'd rescue from a burning house, as they say—we're guessing it probably wouldn't be the mushroom lamp you snagged last year on eBay, or even the vase by that indie ceramicist that you splurged on at a boutique. It would be that rock your friend gave you, or the quilt your grandmother made you when you were a baby, or a chair you grew up with

and eventually inherited. Monica, for example, might choose the paintings she found in the basement of her childhood home that were made by her aunt who died before she was born. Jill would think first of the many special gifts she's been given by designers over the years as thanks for supporting their careers.

Our predisposition toward these physical manifestations of our memories seems to be hardwired into us from birth. As babies, we start to exhibit signs of object attachment, which is the emotional connection we feel to inanimate objects and, conversely, the loss we feel when they're taken away from us. (If you've ever tried to take a blanket or a toy from a small child and triggered a hysterical crying fit, that's object attachment right there.) When we're young, we're fairly indiscriminate about our attachments, though; it could really be any toy or blanket we perceive as "ours." But as we age, these attachments become less about simple possessiveness than about sentiment. You can take any toy away from us now and we won't care too much, but if it's a toy our late grandfather whittled for us when we were seven, we're probably going to protest.

opposite: Wooden nail polish box, 1995. From the collection of Aviva Rowley, whose dad made it for her when she was seven years old.

above: Fledermaus Chair by Josef Hoffmann for Thonet, 1907. From the collection of Monica Khemsurov, who found three thrown out on the street in Manhattan and rehabbed them back to life. Photo courtesy of Rago/Wright.

Stories,
not styles

While sentimental objects are defined by these types of emotional connections, they actually have other, less-obvious merits, too. Because they represent stories and not styles, emotions and not aesthetics, they will always be the most timeless objects you own—the ones you'll never get sick of looking at, that will never make you want to throw out everything you have and redecorate (like the late fashion designer Karl Lagerfeld, who was known for repeatedly decking out his Paris apartment in a single design style before dumping it all at auction and starting over). They are antidotes not only to an overly trendy interior, which we'll talk more about at the end of this chapter, but also to having too much

choice, which is scientifically known to make humans feel unhappy. Just like being handed a restaurant menu that's a mile and a half long, the anxiety of trying to fill a home all at once by selecting from the millions of objects that can be found anywhere on the Internet can be overwhelming enough to make a person give up (or hire a decorator). Whereas if you've had the opportunity to acquire highly meaningful things slowly, over the course of your life, creating your space will always feel more natural, easy, and satisfying.

Since sentimental objects typically can't be purposefully collected or hunted, but come to you more organically, this chapter isn't filled with shopping tutorials like some of the others. However, we can identify the various forms they come in to help you to know them when you see them, and maybe even find ways to encourage their entry into your life. Been up in your parents' attic lately? Time to start rummaging.

Handpainted mask by Park Pardon, 2021. From the collection of Monica Khemsurov, who bought it as a reminder of a mask she had—and lost—as a child.

THE SOUVENIR

Curious travelers have been souvenir-hunting since ancient times, originally for religious objects. These days, the purpose of souvenirs, from fridge magnets to flea-market finds, is to remind you of where you've been, when, and with whom—memories that, because they happened while traveling and taking a break from the stresses of our daily lives, tend to be among the happiest ones we have. "Having the wonderful visual residue of those places is a nice reminder of time you spent outside of yourself," says Singer. "I love buying something when I'm visiting a place not so much because I like to acquire things, but because it becomes this wonderful nostalgic tether."

One of our favorite stories about the strength of our compulsion toward gathering travel mementos comes from the Smithsonian National Museum of American History, whose collection includes a "Plymouth Rock fragment with painted inscription" from 1830. It carries the following description: "In the early 1800s, tourists visiting Plymouth Rock were provided a hammer so that they could take a piece of the rock as a souvenir. By 1880, what was left of the rock was fenced off within a memorial." People were so excited to bring home proof that they'd visited this historic monument that they were willfully *destroying it in the process*! We once read a similar story about Thomas Jefferson and John Adams in the 1700s, slicing off and pocketing bits of wood from one of Shakespeare's chairs while visiting the bard's home in Stratford-upon-Avon. This type of compulsive behavior has actually been quite common throughout history—so common, in fact, that there's a name for its oft-ill-begotten spoils: "piece-of-the-rock" souvenirs, one of the following five categorical classifications proposed by historian Beverly Gordon in her 1986 book, *The Souvenir: Messenger of the Extraordinary.*

- Piece-of-the-rock souvenirs: either natural elements, such as rocks or dried flowers, or actual pieces of something historical, like the Berlin Wall

- Pictorial souvenirs: any type of ephemera, like postcards or posters, that feature images of the destination

- Symbolic souvenirs: a representation of a local icon, such as a miniature Roman Colosseum or Statue of Liberty

- Markers: an object that could have been made anywhere, like a T-shirt or a mug, but is printed with the name or slogan of a place

- Local product souvenirs: food, clothing, or handicrafts that are indigenous to, and ideally made in, a specific region

While most of us have probably dabbled in all of these typologies, because this book is more about decorative objects than historical chunks (or I♥NY T-shirts), the souvenirs we're most interested in fall into the final category: beautiful items that capture something about the place they're from. Sometimes they're one-offs, something we see and just know will always transport us back to a certain city or village in our minds. But some people turn collecting these souvenirs into more of an ongoing activity, deciding on a specific type of item they can look for each time they're away from home, that will vary in unique ways based on where they acquired it. The Los Angeles design gallerist Alex Tieghi-Walker, for example, has a collection of hundreds of small cups—water glasses, espresso cups, etc.—that he's sourced from his extensive travels; every

Vintage glass vase, 1980s. From the collection of Monica Khemsurov, who gifted it to herself on her 40th birthday.

time he goes somewhere, he enjoys searching for the perfect piece to add to his cabinet. He chose cups to collect in the first place because they're usually affordable, and small enough to tuck into a carry-on. But it's also a category with a huge amount of variation, so that a porcelain teacup from England can feel quite English, while a wooden sake cup from Kyoto can be an immediate reminder of Japan.

Unfortunately this kind of culture- or region-specific authenticity is getting harder to find in souvenirs. These days, if you visit the Grand Bazaar in Istanbul, for instance, many of the trinkets you'll see for sale there have been manufactured in other parts of Asia. On a recent stroll through a souvenir-shopping street in Marseille, we noticed that there were at least five stores selling the *same exact* woven bags and speckled ceramics, like they all sourced merchandise from the same mega-wholesaler. In Athens, on the main tourist streets near the Acropolis, you'd be hard pressed to distinguish between any of the leather gladiator sandals or olive-wood bowls and spoons (not always made in Greece either) on offer from the dozens and dozens of shops hawking their wares to foreign visitors.

Before globalization and the Internet, souvenirs used to be the way you could take home a true piece of local culture—an object that was often handmade, and always something totally different from what you could get back home. Back when you couldn't just hop on to Amazon or Alibaba, or even global craft marketplaces like The Citizenry, and find whatever you wanted from wherever you wanted, these items felt exotic and rare, and offered you a window into what life was like in a totally different part of the world. Collectors of these items often displayed them like art. Monica will never forget the time she went to an estate

sale in Washington, D.C., that was lined with faded photographs from the '60s and '70s of a couple on travels to places like Africa and Australia, and jam-packed with displays of the most interesting original artifacts she'd ever seen—such as metal meat skewers topped with elaborate Mesoamerican figures, and intricately hand-carved African masks. She left feeling a strangely intimate connection to these people who clearly led such interesting lives. (She also left with the meat skewers.)

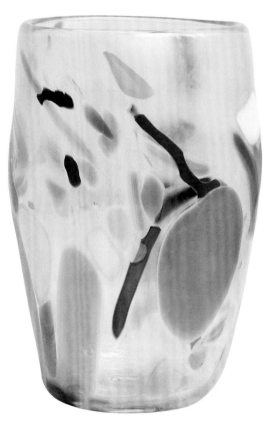

Despite the overall shift from hyperlocal craft objects to anonymous trifles made in far-off factories, high-quality souvenirs—ones that are both memorable and worthy of displaying in your home—are still possible to unearth if you put in a little extra effort. Here are some of our favorite strategies for souvenir shopping.

above: Glass lamp, year unknown. From the collection of Monica Khemsurov, who found the (very heavy) base at a flea market while traveling in Mexico City.

left: Nassau tumblers by Sirius Glassworks, 2013. From the collection of Jill Singer, who received them as a thank-you gift from the designers.

● Attempting to plan our trips around whatever flea market is most well reviewed by locals. Sometimes these markets happen every weekend, and sometimes they're only once a month, so it's important to know before you go. When reading about the market, look carefully for a description of what its wares are like, because while the good ones are primarily for crafts or antiques, others are only for food or for new, cheap, mass-manufactured clothing and housewares.

● Researching the most legitimate artisan workshops or collectives and finding out if they allow visitors. Sometimes a town or city will have a shop (or a market) that sells a curated selection from many different artisans, which is a great starting point. But if you want the best selection, and want a chance to hear the stories behind the objects, it pays to inquire at the shop or market for advice on going straight to the source.

● Similarly, if possible, reaching out to local contemporary artists and designers when you travel somewhere, and asking to pay a visit to their studios. As Singer advises, "talking to people in the community who are cultural producers can lead to other revelations about local culture, and about where they love to go or buy things." You may be able to purchase a great souvenir from them, too.

● Making a point to stop and browse the stands of any object-peddling street vendors you find. "Buying from street vendors is underrated," says Wu. "In certain places in the world, that's how you meet the person who's like, 'I just came from my village with this selection of stuff, and it's made by a community of women.' Also, when you don't buy the typical for-tourist items from them, it's an encouragement for them to pursue the more authentic or unusual thing they weren't sure was going to sell."

Singer, who's something of a souvenir-collecting fanatic, has filled her own home with the spoils of these types of activities. "I'm looking around my house and seeing the beautiful pitcher I got in Bulgaria, and the brass bowl I got at a dirt market in Georgia," she says. "In 2020, I traveled around Colombia with a friend from Bogotá, visiting artisans and little shops supporting local makers. I have a basket from Cartageña and a pillow that has an Anni Albers–style weaving pattern that's indigenous to the area." Most of her finds, she says, come from flea markets and antique shops. "I always do the research before, to find out, for example, what is *the* antique store in Puglia. It takes a lot of digging and might be something you find on some random blog." It's all worth it, though, when you score something good, and the extra effort you put in makes the objects you take home all the more meaningful. The hidden gems are always the ones you remember most.

Lacquered nautilus shell table, year unknown. From the collection of designer and Florida-based vintage dealer Kelsey Heinze, who drove 10 hours to buy this table, which had been custom-made for the seller's mother.

above left: Filippa candlesticks by Kjell Engman for Kosta Boda, 1989. From the collection of Jill Singer, who bought them to commemorate Sight Unseen's first designed product for the home—a rug for Kasthall.

above right: Untitled (10 Cubes) by Vasa Mihich, 1983. From the collection of Monica Khemsurov, who grew up coveting her uncle's set. Photo courtesy of Rago/Wright.

left: Salt and pepper shakers by C. Jorgensen, 1987. From the collection of Aviva Rowley, who loved Jorgensen's designs since she was a kid.

opposite: Vintage umbrella lamp, year unknown. From the collection of dealer Sadie Perry, who sees it as an extension of her personality—it's one of the few things she won't sell.

THE HEIRLOOM

If the objects you've inherited (or stand to inherit) look anything like the ones pictured in this book, you're lucky. Most of us have families who either never owned anything that nice, never owned anything that suited our tastes, or owned nice things but got rid of them over the years. Jill falls into the second category—though her parents' sofa embroidered with tropical birds and cherry blossoms was a definite statement!—while Monica falls into the third. Her family never had fancy things, but they did have strangely cool ones that mysteriously disappeared along the way, like a 1970s fabric wall piece depicting a hand pouring water from a Perrier bottle and a Modernist plaster sculpture on a plinth. Neither of her parents knows what happened to them.

New York design gallerist Lora Appleton of Kinder Modern immediately came to mind when we started thinking about family heirlooms: She lives with a trove of them, most passed down from her grandmother, who was a painter, sculptor, and collector of beautiful things. In Appleton's Tribeca home—the contents of which, she notes, are all sentimental in some way— stone sculptures by her grandma sit side-by-side with pieces by contemporary designers she's worked with and pinch-pots by her thirteen-year-old son. "I have in front of me right now five of my grandmother's sculptures, which I remember running my hands over as a child," she says. "I also have a kinetic sculpture that lived in my grandfather's office when I was a kid. I have a lot of memories attached to these things. The people I associate them with are gone, and the objects are all I have left. It's like a cocoon or a cloak for me: I'm wrapped in my history through those pieces. Some of my grandmother's works still smell like her. I like having her near me."

To Appleton's point, inherited objects, of course, are so much more than just things you get to own without paying for them. They might summon extremely strong, visceral evocations of people or spaces you once knew, or of your family's culture or traditions. If Monica's parents had kept that 1970s Perrier artwork and she'd hung it up in the kitchen of her New York apartment, it wouldn't be because she liked it better than any other art she could afford to buy. It would be because whenever she looked at it she'd remember all the times as a kid that she'd leap out of bed the morning of her birthday and excitedly pull up a chair underneath it to unwrap the presents her parents had piled on the kitchen table. That experience of reliving the past—and sharing those childhood stories with guests—would have been so much more interesting than living with the print she has on the wall now, which she ordered from an online store.

It's stylish, but it simply fades into the background noise of her daily life.

Perhaps the most interesting aspect of living with heirlooms, though, is how they can be impregnated with stories of not just your own life but those of your ancestors. Appleton has a collage by Barbara Kruger that holds the tale of how Kruger and her grandmother developed a friendship, traded artworks, and then how her grandmother altered Kruger's piece by pasting her own cut-out words over ones the artist had originally used. Objects can reference the lives our grandparents lived before they immigrated, or the rituals they participated in, or the travels they or our parents did before we were born. The same way that history used to be passed down from generation to generation through oral storytelling, these objects can become vessels for keeping those histories alive.

Unfortunately we can't offer much guidance on how to acquire heirlooms—you either inherit them or you don't. But there are a few ways to make sure you don't miss the opportunity to welcome them into your home. If there's a piece you love in the living room of a family member you have a *really* good relationship with, and they don't seem attached to the object themselves, perhaps you can offer to replace it with a more functional, contemporary equivalent (I buy you a nice new clock, you give me the one that I find meaningful). To seek out objects that might be more up for grabs, offer to help a family member organize their garage or attic. It might be full of golf clubs and tax records, but if they have great taste or a storied past, it might hold unexpected surprises.

And if all else fails, you can always adopt strangers' heirlooms. "My other grandparents took me to estate sales starting when I was eight, and I was sentimental about people's old things," laughs Appleton. "I could imagine the story behind them, and feel that energetic connection."

opposite: Stone sculpture by Barbara Gross, 1976. From the collection of Lora Appleton, Gross's granddaughter, who grew up around her art.

THE GIFT

When we're young, we love getting gifts for purely transactional and materialistic reasons—we want more things, and feel a primal sense of reward whenever they're handed to us. But as adults, the value of a gift becomes much more abstract: it's usually the notion that someone was thinking about us in the moment that they bought it, made it, or picked it up that feels the most gratifying. If the gift happens to be just right, that gratification is amplified with the even more profound feeling of being truly seen or understood by another person, a symbolism so strong we're likely to associate it with that object for life. That's why, on the scale of positive energy levels that objects can radiate into a room, the gift is among the highest—even if it's from someone we met only briefly but who had reason to thank or acknowledge us. As Wu puts it, "We want our objects to remind us of the times when we were at our best." Gifts, she says, represent the instances "when we were generous to others, or they were generous to us; when we managed to connect with someone."

Leaving out more functional gifts like headphones or novelty socks, a sentimental object–type gift can take many forms: a shell brought back from a friend's vacation, a fan-shaped vase snagged for you at a flea market because you love everything Art Deco, a piece of art made for you for your birthday, a ceramic cup given to you to mark the end of a creative collaboration. The handmade ones tend to be the most touching, because part of the gift is knowing the amount of work and care the gift-giver put into making it on your behalf. Not to mention knowing you've been given something no one else has. In our own homes, when we have guests over who comment on our collections, we particularly love telling the stories behind those objects, as a small way of crediting the maker's generosity. One of our favorites is a set of five candlesticks the Brooklyn design studio Fort Standard made for us on the occasion of Sight Unseen's fifth birthday. Each candlestick featured a differently shaped white oak body turned on a lathe, topped with a cylinder of brass, and weighted with a base of white or black marble. They're beautiful design objects in their own right, but they're also infused with meaning because of our shared history as friends and colleagues.

For Wu, the majority of her vast personal collection comprises objects she's been gifted by artists or designers as thanks for writing about their work, including them in an exhibition, or visiting their studio and getting to know them. But for those who don't have similar opportunities, the best chance of welcoming more gifts into your life is, of course, to give more of them to others. The key is to buy or make them in the moment, when you happen to come across or think of something that reminds you of someone else, rather than waiting for a special occasion to go looking for something perfect. That way you capture the most genuine, potent feeling in the gift, something people really notice.

Spanish tile from Casa de Pilatos, 16th century. From the collection of Martha Mulholland, who considers it a memento from the trip to Spain during which her husband proposed.

Wu shared with us an approach to reciprocal gift-giving that we found especially inspiring: She and her best friends build ongoing collections for one another based on private references and inside jokes. "With my friend Kimberly, I always give her rocks that look like food, and she always gives me things shaped like clams," Wu says. "It makes shopping more pleasurable, and whenever I find something, I can save it for the next milestone—here's your wedding present, your birthday present, and your anniversary present, forever. I love having a personal list of things I'm always looking for that are related to people I love."

This type of arrangement is also a great way to avoid the more unfortunate side of gifts, which is when you get one that's thoughtful, but just really doesn't suit your taste or your interior. Wu advocates for adding them to your collection anyway: "It's just so nice to have your world expanded by other people, through these things," she says. "It makes your home a little less like a theme. You can incorporate all these other perspectives."

OEE Bowl by Jeroen van de Gruiter, 2017. From the collection of Monica Khemsurov, who received it as a gift from the designer.

SENTIMENTAL OBJECTS AT HOME

They say your taste in food changes every seven years. Your taste in interiors, we'd guess every three to eight. (Or if you run a design magazine, like we do, every one to three.) The benefit of incorporating sentimental objects into your space is that, since their appeal is more emotional than aesthetic, you won't get sick of them the way you might that squiggly mirror you saw all over Instagram four years ago. Even when they do happen to be both memorable and visually appealing, these objects often have little to do with a specific era, style, or trend. And if you break up a trend-driven interior with timeless, meaningful objects, your home will feel more unique and less like an influencer's Pinterest board.

We won't deny that it can be challenging to incorporate items you're emotionally tied to into an interior they don't necessarily suit. But, like Wu, we think it's worth making the effort—perhaps by finding other ways to make connections between your objects besides just a certain uniform look. Maybe you're telling a story about natural materials and craftsmanship, or thinking of your home like a cabinet of curiosities. Wu explains her own approach: "I want to look back on my life and reflect upon it as one of friendship and serendipity and kindness, so it's the sentimental items I surround myself with, and everything in between is more of an aesthetic thing," she says. "But the fact that they both mix easily in my home is because I tend to be friends with people with whom I share similar philosophical inclinations about stuff, and who appreciate the handmade. Those are ideas that carry through my objects, even when they're given to me by different people."

Luckily, it's a great moment for eclecticism: In the current interiors zeitgeist, you actually get extra credit for incorporating weird visual and period-based incongruities into your space. Maybe your living room is outfitted with serious Modernist furniture, but you have a pair of wacky ceramic candlesticks your best friend made you on a shelf, and your family's silver clock from the 1700s on the mantel. While the 1700s aren't currently trending, it works because it's meaningful to you, and as such, becomes its own kind of unexpected statement.

And of course if you join one thing that feels out of

place with five other things that do, too, it starts to feel like a more intentional moment.

We'll talk more about these methods in our final chapter, on styling, but if you walk away with one piece of inspiration from this chapter, let it be that the most effortlessly stylish people—with the most effortlessly stylish interiors—don't just follow along with what everyone else thinks looks cool. They instinctively disrupt it with the pieces they really love, without even thinking twice. If looking at a special object every day makes you feel good, then that's the object you should display. If it's not an obvious choice, that only makes it a more interesting one.

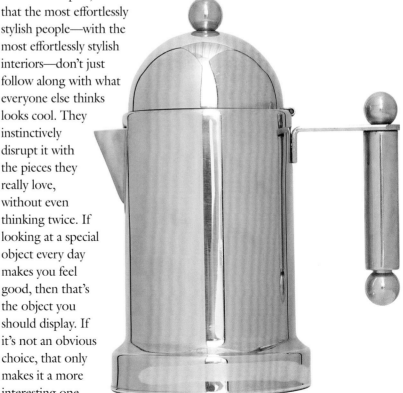

above: Vintage Vev Viganò Kontessa milk jug, 1980s. From the collection of Jill Singer, who received the three-part coffee service as a gift from her husband.

opposite: Shifting Shape Vase by Jonatan Nilsson, 2017. From the collection of Jill Singer, who stumbled upon Nilsson's work during a particularly memorable trip to Stockholm.

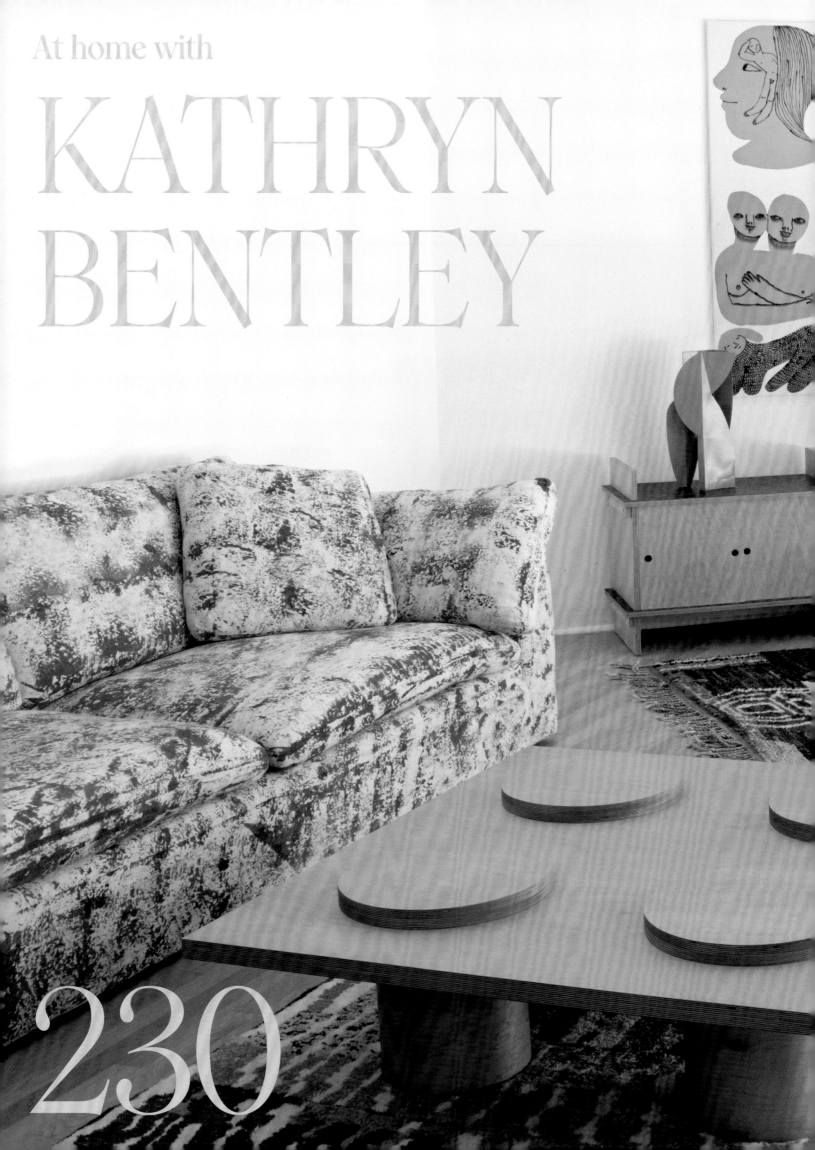

At home with

KATHRYN BENTLEY

230

Bentley is the founder of Dream Collective, a fine jewelry line and erstwhile boutique in Los Angeles, where she sold work by an enviable lineup of contemporary designers, including Morgan Peck, Ben Medansky, Peter Shire, Bari Ziperstein, and Shin Okuda. Her 1920s Spanish-style home, which she shares with her partner, Jen, and their four-year-old son, Gus, includes former shop pieces, work she's commissioned from friends, ceramics she's traded her own jewelry for, and mementos she's inherited from her eighty-year-old father, an artist and architect.

" Our Emma Kohlmann painting, to me, represents our family. It's happy, and just a lighter approach to art than what I normally would want or be attracted to. Less serious. At one point, my four-year-old's drawings were surrounding all of the art on the wall and it actually looked even better—a more casual take on fine art. That painting arrived mid-COVID, when all of a sudden, I had become a teacher and was needing to create activities. I felt like it was nice to be able to have these inspiring pieces around." ←

" I don't think I consciously decided that I was only going to have pieces in my home by people I know, but it made sense because I happen to have such talented friends. There was a minute before I had kids where I actually bought several pieces from the gallerist Eve Fowler just because she was cool and part of the queer community. But most of the things in my house are definitely by people I know, like this Peter Shire sculpture." →

" Shin Okuda from Waka Waka has been a friend of mine since I moved to LA. I'm so glad I held on to at least one piece of his. The coffee table is so playful in that room because it's like a giant Lego. It's usually covered in trains and books."

"I got the Restoration Hardware Cloud Sofa after seeing Pamela Shamshiri use it in several of her interiors. It sat there in its pure white canvas form for about a year, and for a while, I just hated it. It didn't feel like me. When I had the Dream Collective shop, I had been doing all of this textile printing—I made pillows and sofa cushions for pieces by Shin from Waka Waka—and finally I was like, I have to do this to my sofa. It could be totally hideous and I might ruin this several-thousand-dollar couch, or it might be great. Over the summer, I went for it. I brought all the cushions to my studio and got the fabric paint and rollers and some loose sponges and went to town. Then I sent it to the dye house to have the dye fixed, and it turned out great. At first I thought it was too much, but I can't imagine having a different couch now."

"On the wall in the dining room is a piece by Jennie Jieun Lee, and on the Mario Bellini Colonnato table are pieces by Morgan Peck, Cody Hoyt, Peter Shire, and Bari Ziperstein, among others. Bari and I became super close over the last few years, and I traded a ton of jewelry for her ceramics. She's been something of a mentor to me, in terms of life and art and running a business from the ground up. She gave me that thumbprint piece for my fortieth birthday, which I thought was kind of funny because it's an urn. One day, I'll end up in a Bari Ziperstein, which, in a way, she knew I would want. I don't want to be left in just any old urn! Now I'm prepared to go out in style." →

"Before I moved into this house with Jen, I had always lived in really contemporary spaces. My dad was an architect, and I grew up in houses he built. My last house before this one, in Montecito Heights, was a blank slate—'60s minimal mid-century. So, moving into this 1920s Spanish style, I really had to open my mind. I had to strip down a lot, but also accept the embellishments that come along with that era of architecture. Obviously, I have a more contemporary style and I'm attracted to contemporary furniture more than would be appropriate for this space."

"My dream was to have my dad build a house for me, but having his sculptures is the next best thing. He's eighty years old, and he's always made art alongside his architecture, but he also recently started making these paper maquettes that he turns into sculpture. He sits at his desk and folds beautiful pieces of thick paper, and then he goes down to this sheet metal place in Texas and instructs the guys on how to fold each piece in metal. The first one he gave me was the blue one below. The cream piece on the chest of drawers at right was made specifically to represent our family; he told us this story about how each piece represented me and Jen and Gus. I couldn't live without them. They each hold such a presence for me and it's just nice to have a little piece of him in my house."

At home with

TATJANA VON STEIN & GAYLE NOONAN

240

Partners in both life and work, **von Stein and Noonan** cofounded the full-service creative studio Sella Concept, with von Stein in charge of interior architecture and furniture design and Noonan handling branding and identity. The pair live in a London town house with breathtaking top-floor views and they've filled it with quirky pieces they've collected as well as relics of past projects they've done together.

66 Our objects are a mix of pieces we've bought in vintage markets, pieces we've made, and pieces we've collected from artists we love and respect. It's this random mix of collectibles and emotive pieces that Tatjana's trying to introduce more of into Sella Studio's interiors projects. The secretary in the living room, for example, Tatjana inherited from her grandmother, which somehow brings her grandmother's wisdom and love into our home. It sits right next to a painting by Gayle and the first and only sculpture Tatjana ever made, on a night course as a teenager, surrounded by mothers complaining about their teenage daughters."

66 This stool is the first furniture piece Tatjana designed. It was based on the bathers' shapes and forms in the ladies' pond in Hampstead Heath, which is the neighborhood we now live in." ←

> Gayle loves negative space, while Tatjana is always gently and discreetly introducing little finds. We came to a firm agreement that our bedroom would stay nothing but serene. Furniture and objects seem to be like people to us, our little friends around the house that make us smile." →

“ We love this room. It's gold—what were we thinking?—yet calm and indulgent. It reminds us of so many moments, like Gayle surprising Tatjana with this gorgeous print by Victor Pasmore, who's her favorite British expressionist. The linen curtains are from a set we built on a Netflix job, and the lamp is Shiro Kuramata's Shogun lamp for Artemide. The Art Deco wardrobe is about to explode open because of our coat obsession."

We first met while creating a concept store for a client. We both visited Akari's pottery studio, and little did we know that we would get married three years later and the piece would end up sitting on our dining table, which Tatjana recently designed. This scene also depicts much more, such as Gayle's love for this strange little porcelain apple, Tatjana's uncle's plinth, the first floor lamp Tatjana ever bought herself, and José, our cactus (who has other overgrown friends in the living space, named Hervé, among others)."

At home with

SU
WU

'248

A writer and curator, **Wu** rose to prominence as founder of the influential blog I'm Revolting, which unearthed unusual and often anonymous designs. Now based in Mexico City with her husband, the artist Alma Allen, and their two children, Wu is a staunch champion of the local design scene, using her home—a converted community theater—as a place to co-curate exhibitions and showcase her ever-growing collection of gifts, Mexican crafts, and contemporary art and design.

" The house was built in the 1920s in the Roma Norte neighborhood, and it used to be a community theater. There was a mirrored room; I found videos later on YouTube of little kids having jazz class in here. There was a black box theater with risers. There are little odd-shaped windows that you can tell were for projectors. One of the balconies has a section cut out of it, which I think must've been for when they swung things across the stage."

"The huge ceramic chalice under the red Michael Rey sculpture is by Kathleen Ryan. I bought it at a ceramics sale, and then two years later, she happened to visit Alma's studio. She was like, 'Oh my gosh, where did this piece come from? That's the first piece I ever sold.' Now she makes these big fruits that look like they're rotting, with semi-precious stones covering them. Her work is interested in this idea of luxury, and what an amazing life we have that we can let fruit rot and go to waste. But this was part of an early series. At the show, there was a wine fountain pouring into it."

" The bread sculpture on the wall makes me think of my friend Carmen. We had a project together called Club Sandwich, and we would host potlucks where you were asked to bring a single sandwich. It's actually by a French artist named Vincent Olinet, but it feels like a Carmen piece. It's my cell phone charging spot now."

" I'm drawn to things that feel like they have a lot of experiment in their making— like the person was working through something or figuring something out. For example, the chair at the end of the entry hall is by José Pérez Garza, a young carpenter from Monterrey. He tried to make a Shaker chair having never seen one! In general, I'm really interested in how non-European, non-US designers interpret European and American design tropes. It's the reverse of Modernist appropriation, and I feel like it's an indication of a new shift in thinking, power dynamics, and privilege, and who gets to play around with ideas."

"I'm lucky because we have a lot of things that were made by Alma—early pieces that he made while he was figuring out his voice and his style. This has become a joke between Alma and me— that we have what no one else would buy. He's always like, 'You need to stop bringing home the first thing that a person ever made,' but that, apparently, is what I'm really drawn to."

"Everything on the table is by Alma except the lamp, which is by Ron Rezek. The rubber table is by Brian Thoreen, a really good friend. I don't know if it was a gift. We did a Masa Galeriá show here, and this piece was in it, and it sort of just stayed. I don't want to call it a gift and have Brian be like, 'No, it's not!' There's absolutely no hardware, so it's held together entirely by the weight of its own material. It's perfect."

"On the right side of this shelf, there are two little flaming figures. I first saw them in the house of the photographer Graciela Iturbide. They're lost souls in purgatory, on fire, and I loved how the representation of fire is so hilarious and interpretive. I looked and looked for them, and I finally found them one day at this antique shop. As I was going to pay for them, the guy started yelling, 'Get out!' I felt like I had offended him, but then I realized there was an earthquake siren going off. I ran out and never went back for them. Years later, I was having lunch with my friend Dung Ngo, and he told me he'd stopped at this antique shop on the way here. I told him the story, and then was like, 'What did you get?' He said, 'Oh my god, I got the souls in purgatory.' I really did feel a pang! But he sensed it, and he gave them to me, which was the sweetest thing. It takes a special person to realize how important things will be to you."

"Everything in my home is something that's from a friend or that I found with a friend or that I associate with a story of a friend. The little wooden chair in the atrium is by Jardín, which is two designers from Mexico City, Roberto Michelsen and Carmen Cantu Artigas. It was a gift from them, which was very sweet. What I love about prototypes or gifts is that they really embody a certain freedom. I think some designers and artists struggle with wanting to make work for themselves without having to be overly concerned about the audience. These things are made for just one person." ↑

"The bathroom wall was entirely designed by our carpenter. I wanted something that felt a little bit more traditionally Mexican, and this is what he came up with—which, I was like, huh, okay. There's actually a gigantic vent hiding behind it that goes to the ceiling, because we thought, for a moment, that we might open up a restaurant in the space. The tile was just me going to the tile shop and being that weird person who's there for way too long laying things out. It's traditional Mexican Talavera tile." ←

MY FAVORITE THING

What makes an object sentimental has less to do with the object itself than with the personal circumstances surrounding its acquisition. To one person, a pair of candlesticks might simply be something they bought at a boutique before hosting a big dinner party; to another, those same candlesticks might have outsized significance as the last gift their partner gave them before a breakup. When we first started Sight Unseen, it was our primary mission to capture the stories behind the making of our favorite designs, but truthfully, we find all kinds of stories about objects compelling, including the ones that offer a glimpse into what happens once they find their way out in the world and into people's lives. Here, seven object enthusiasts share a possession that's particularly meaningful to them, as well as the story of how it acquired such an exaggerated sense of worth.

258

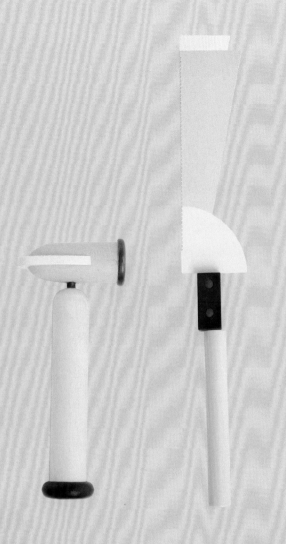

Ellen Van Dusen

designer, Dusen Dusen, New York City

"My friend Tasha, who lives in California, found this color-blocked knife at a flea market and gave it to me as a gift. I was using it as a bread knife, but it's very bad at cutting bread. It basically tears it to shreds. Then, a couple of years ago, I saw that my friend Steven Bukowski had posted a photo of it on Instagram as part of a larger set that included two screwdrivers, a hammer, and some nails. I was like, 'Holy shit, this isn't a knife. It's a saw!' I don't think the designer was technically affiliated with the Memphis design movement, but he'd called it Memphis Toolkit. Maybe it was a marketing technique; maybe it was an homage. I still don't know that much about him. But I thought, 'What a joy to have a knife/saw that looks so silly.'

Later, I was at my parents' house, and I found the matching hammer in my brother's old bedroom. It was kind of beat up, and it was clear that we'd all used it as kids. But I took it—without asking anyone for permission—and now I have two out of the five pieces in the set. It's so funny, because when I first got the knife, I wouldn't have known where to start in identifying it. There's no branding on it. And if I'd tried to Google 'funky bread knife,' I wouldn't have gotten anywhere, because obviously, it's a saw."

Athena Calderone

interior designer, New York City

"This green marble head was in my home growing up in Long Island. My parents weren't big collectors of objects or design, and they didn't have many pieces that I'd feel connected to now. But I always remembered this one. My dad was a hairdresser, and this sculpture was given to him as a gift from a client. A few years ago, when he became unwell and had to move into an assisted living facility, I put his things in storage, and when I came upon it, all of these memories of my childhood came flooding back.

Growing up, I always thought she was super beautiful. Even though we're not Greek—we're Italian—I thought of her as this Grecian goddess. She felt really mysterious and regal to me. Now, as an adult, this sculpture touches on so many things I love about design. One of my design philosophies is to create both contrast and cohesion, and I feel like it does both; it has a softness and elegance, but it feels slick and harsh at the same time, so there's a tension.

Finding it in my dad's things also happened to coincide with when I was first designing my town house, so it was almost like she reappeared at the perfect time, when I was seeking out pieces that trigger memories or that have a story. I'm such a believer in curation and the thought that objects are imbued with a history and memories. This piece felt like the perfect thing, rooted in family history, to add to my home.

My mom always joked that perhaps the client gave my dad a two-faced woman because he's a Gemini with a split personality. But that's just my mom being cheeky."

Alison Roman
food writer and chef, New York City

" I went home to LA recently, and when I was there, I went to this awesome antique furniture store called Just One Eye and fell in love with this bowl. I've been going through an amber glass phase for a long time—maybe because it seems to be one of the only colored glasses that's a little less trendy—and I've never seen anything like it. The texture is almost ropelike; it has this twist at the foot that I was completely captivated by. Anyway, this was my first trip home with my boyfriend after we started dating, and he was like, 'I would like to buy this for you.' I was like, 'Uh, I can buy it myself,' but he was like, 'No, I want to.' So, I let him buy it for me.

I love bowls, and I have a lot of them. Ornate glass bowls are not particularly practical to cook with, so this is just decorative. I love the way it looks on my burl-wood dining table, especially at a certain time of day. It's a sunset bowl! There's also a '70s energy to it, which I'm really attracted to. It reminds me of my great-aunt Miriam, who was the first woman travel agent in Beverly Hills. She and her husband were very well-off, and her house had these insane original teak floors, a pool table with beaded curtains, and a mahogany, teak-y vibe. In one room, there was this curtain with big amber beads. She and my grandma were always very into collecting *objets* and bric-a-brac, too, so I think I must have always been interested in that on some level.

Because of what I do, my home and my kitchen are photographed pretty frequently, and to me, it's really important that I have individuality. I don't want the same shit that everyone else has. Everyone has this cutting board, everyone has these knives—it contributes to the homogenous nature of photographs and social media and art. I'm not flexing, like 'Look at my cool thrifted items.' But a photograph will inherently look different with these bowls or plates or vases. Not everything in my apartment is vintage or thrifted. But the important things are."

Lykke Li
musician, Los Angeles

" Before I had my baby in 2016 and bought a house in LA, I'd been touring for ten years, and kept an apartment in Stockholm that was basically empty—it only had a bed and some books in it. I had no furniture. When I got the house, I finally felt adult enough to buy a table, and I fell in love with this one. It's a piece of sculpture. It's the most unpractical table there is because it's so heavy, but I only buy furniture for its beauty and craftsmanship, not necessarily for comfort or practicality. And I'd rather have nothing than buy something temporary. I was also really interested in Gae Aulenti; she was really radical. I love to collect furniture pieces that are classic but, at the time they were made, were quite progressive and modern.

When I bought the table six years ago, it seemed like a crazy purchase. It was an astronomical sum for me, especially because I'd only ever really bought a mattress before. It felt a bit like I was going through a midlife crisis, like when a man buys a sports car. But then I realized something. I'm always searching for perfection and symmetry—dissecting my songs all day long, or spending a lot of time looking at angles in my house that bother me, wishing it was a little more like this or like that. Yet with this piece, Aulenti clearly thought about the angles, the structures, and the choices for so long. I can look at it and it makes me so calm. It gives me a sense of symmetry in the chaos. A sense that some things actually do last forever."

Misha Kahn

designer, New York City

    I found this shell vase at a flea market in Medellín when I was visiting a designer friend in Colombia. Everything else in the market was very obviously handicraft or a vintage item or some junky secondhand thing. This felt like the odd thing out. Someone had clearly made it with love. The color choice is both insane and oddly contemporary. The shells are applied with mortar or concrete, but it's so thick; it doesn't feel like they were trying to glue shells to the outside, it feels like they were trying to build a whole wall.

A lot of times when you travel, there's such an industry around craft that even if you're not buying the obvious tourist thing, it's still related. I'm always looking for the rogue deviant. I got it before the whole peak–shell interiors trend, but I do have a soft spot for shell interiors.

Now that the vase is home, I use it as a planter. It floats in the middle of the room on a stool that I made, and there's a little aloe plant that fits into it perfectly. I like that it's so close to being normal but then so far as well. I feel like it could almost have been on Sight Unseen. Like sometimes I make assemblages with concrete, too, in this similar vein of putting together a scrappy object. But it would never occur to me to then paint the whole thing the brightest blue. It's such a goofy enigma of an object."

Mel Ottenberg

editor-in-chief, *Interview* magazine, New York City

"Many years ago, I moved in with my now ex-boyfriend and we got the late Jim Walrod to design our apartment—both so that we could live a fantasy lifestyle and also so that we wouldn't kill each other over all of the furniture decisions. I'd bought a dining table and couch, and found the perfect lighting fixtures, but then I was like, 'Okay, what's going *on* the dining table?' I had all of these ideas that were probably too complicated and definitely wrong, and Jim said, 'You need the Ettore Sottsass Murmansk bowl. It's the only thing.' But I had sticker shock—it's insanely beautiful, but rare, expensive, and not an impulse kind of buy. I would text him pictures of other options, and he was always like *no*. Six months later I would try again, and he was like, 'No, just get the Murmansk.'

One day, I was at the Memphis show at the Met Breuer and there was the Murmansk, sitting on a pedestal. I sent Jim a pic, and even my mom sent me a photo from the show saying, 'You really should get this.' And I still didn't get it! This went on for a while, and unfortunately Jim passed away, gone too soon, and I broke up with my boyfriend. Finally, I was like, 'What are you doing?' Yes, it costs money, but it's also amazing, and it's important to have because someone I really cared about, who cared about me, really wanted me to have it. I ended up buying it for myself as a breakup prize. It really is the right thing—the only thing that should ever be on my dining table. Now, years later, I'm bored of other things in my interior, but there's no world in which the Murmansk isn't my exact personality. It's hardcore, it's silver, it's unique, and you either get it or you don't. And it's the only thing on my table, besides a plastic singing pickle that my brother gave me for Christmas. A yodeling pickle, my Murmansk fruit bowl, and that's it."

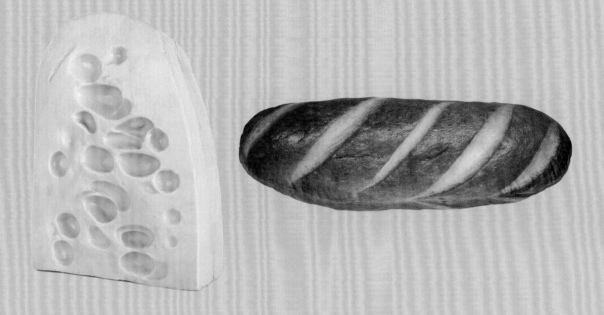

Matylda Krzykowski
design curator and critic, Berlin

" It started with the cheese. I live above a vintage lamp shop in Berlin, and I pass by it every day. One day there was one difference—there was a plastic cheese in the window. I always wondered, 'Why is there a cheese among the lamps?' I liked the randomness of it, how the cheese disturbed the lights but also added something. Finally, I went into the shop and asked the guy if he'd sell me the cheese, and he said, 'Sure, give me twenty euros. But where will you put it?' I said I was thinking of putting it in my kitchen, and he said, 'Okay, but *don't accidentally grate the cheese!*' I like how it looks like a sculpture, and how it has attitude. The way it's shaped, somehow it looks full of pride.

The bread I found when I initially wanted to buy a bed pillow. When I was Googling pillows, the algorithm immediately suggested this one. I was distracted from the idea of an actual sleeping pillow, and now I just had to have the bread. Once I received it, it became almost like a person—I'd have him sitting upright on the ground, or on a chair, or lying down. A photographer friend of mine was staying with me at the time, and we started calling him Bready and photographing him wearing sunglasses, or a bikini. I'd come home and Bready would be sitting on my bed in lingerie. It has the shape of a character; both of these objects are characters, in a way. Characters of my interior.

People make things or ideas into objects because we want to be reminded of something. I love cheese and bread. And I like objects that aren't on a normal scale. You could produce actual bread and cheese in this size, but you couldn't keep them. They'd have an expiration date, but the pillow and sculpture don't expire. They last. And why can't we live with food forever?"

266

Harvey Guzzini Olympe Lamp for ED, 1970s, in
the London home of Charlotte Taylor

STYLING

There's a reason we chose the word "styling" as the title of
our final chapter: Whereas "decorating" refers to creating a
holistic vision for a space at the macro level, with the objects
acting as supporting characters in a larger story, "styling"
is more about how you arrange things at the micro level,
creating moments and vignettes that highlight the objects
in the most interesting and aesthetically pleasing ways.
You decorate a room; you style a shelf. While the
most aspirational interiors admittedly nail both, there are
plenty of books about decorating out there, and this isn't
one of them. If you're truly an object lover, focusing your
efforts around your favorite possessions may feel like
second nature anyway: "I've never opened a decorating
magazine for inspiration in my life," says Linda Meyers of
Wary Meyers. "First we find something, and then we create
a space to organize it or display it. The interior is created
to house the cool objects. You want to show them off—even
just to yourself."

Here, we'll be sharing our own general thoughts about
how to successfully incorporate your objects into your
interior, as well as asking a few experts and homeowners
for their best insider tips. The upside of this approach is
that, unlike decorating advice, which is subject more to the
whims of what's fashionable at any given time, styling advice
is about spatial positioning and other concepts that exist
outside the realm of trends, so these are ideas you can use for
years—or decades—to come.

BASIC STYLING PRINCIPLES

Letting objects breathe

As Meyers said, when you really love your objects—and have invested time and energy into procuring really great ones—you want to show them off. And the best way to show them off properly is to give them a little breathing room, so they look as singular and as prominent as possible, and can make a greater visual impact. "I wouldn't call myself a minimalist, but I think things need space around them to be properly appreciated," the London design writer Tom Morris once told the blog

The Modern House. This doesn't mean that you can't create clusters of objects where they do make sense, like a grouping of five modern vases with a similar lava finish, but if you have an especially standout piece, you'll want to highlight it by giving it unobstructed views and not associating it too closely with another object that could influence the way it's perceived. This may mean that you have to make tough choices about how to allocate your shelf or table space if it's limited, but that's an important part of the process, too. "In Donald Judd's interiors, he only brought an object in as it was needed, and as it could hold the space," notes Friedman Benda's Alex Gilbert. "That's a nice philosophy. You have to bring new things into your space consciously."

Juxtaposing and layering

If you want the objects in your home to be entirely mid-century, or entirely Postmodern, we aren't going to tell you any different. But most of us can't help loving objects of all different types and aesthetics, at which point the fundamental question of styling becomes a question of how to make them all play nicely together, in visual harmony. That's where the concepts of juxtaposition and layering come in—confidently mixing the natural with the manmade, the vintage with the contemporary, the organic with the linear. There's no one way to do this; it relies on finding other types of visual connections, like shape or color, and trying things out until you find a combination that works. But the bottom line is that layering disparate types of objects and artworks together is a good thing, and will make your interiors look more sophisticated and thoughtful. Gilbert keeps a megalodon tooth mounted on the wall next to her best artworks. Kinder Modern's Lora Appleton will place a $1 find from a flea market alongside a work by an emerging maker. "There's a conversation that happens between them," she says. "The mix of even having an object next to a plant, and how that changes the scale or the feeling of something—I think that's how we live now."

Custom coffee table by Elliot Barnes in the London home of Raphaël Zerbib

Finding balance

Whether your objects are similar or different, clustered together or spread out and singular, deciding on their exact spatial placement in a room or on a table is all about creating the most harmonious visual balance, where items displayed near each other don't look completely out of scale, and one side of a room or a mantel doesn't feel too heavy or crowded compared to the other side. A 24-inch-tall vase will often look better next to a 16-inch-tall sculpture than a 2-inch-tall paperweight, for example, and if you have one area where your objects are very evenly spaced out and symmetrical, the neighboring area might benefit from being more asymmetrical. There are some rules of thumb you can use to find visual balance—interior designer Keren Richter once described her approach to styling bookshelves as "triangulation," where a visually prominent object on one shelf can be balanced by two less visually prominent objects placed on the shelf below it—but the process relies mostly on looking carefully, using your intuition, and being attuned to the ways your objects can complement rather than fight one another.

Repositioning and repurposing

When you've played around with the styling of your objects for a while and have found a configuration that really works, it can be tempting to leave everything exactly as it is, in perpetuity. But who wants to live in a museum? The point of incorporating objects into your home is that they help breathe life and personality into your space, and that entails letting things change and evolve as your interests change, or even just in a moment when you feel like creating new energy in a room. The process should be fun and flexible, not stuffy and static. "We have a picture rail around our dining room that we use for objects," says Gilbert. "I'll wake up one Sunday morning and my husband will have been up late rearranging everything. The next weekend, I'll do it. Not being so preconceived about the placement of our objects is really liberating. Even for large items like the sofa—you might surprise yourself by flipping it and having it face the windows instead." Allowing yourself the freedom to revisit your object placements on a whim also makes it easier to incorporate new things, and to repurpose old ones: Instead of getting rid of a vase that isn't working on the dining table, you might recontextualize it by moving it to the bathroom instead.

A collection of objects in the Mexico City home of Su Wu

The art of the edit

If the question of how much is too much were easy to answer, Marie Kondo wouldn't have built a multimillion-dollar empire around answering it. When your objects all carry meanings and memories, though, the process gets even harder—do our John Hogan glass paperweights bring us joy? Of course, but so do the forty other objects gunning for our limited shelf space. Forcing yourself to edit, though, is a critical part of the styling process, because it's the only way to ensure that the objects you do display have enough space to shine. The first step is to address the amount of objects you acquire in the first place. Can you post a photo of that new find instead of buying it? Can you think of where you'll put it if you do bring it home? If not, says Meyers, you might want to pass it by. Her rule while vintage shopping is, "If it doesn't have a home, it's not allowed to roam," she says. Second, you have to decide how much to display in a certain room or area so that it looks layered but not cluttered. Our stylist experts will weigh in on that shortly, but a general rule is that shelves can be about quantity, but surfaces should be about quality, so keep those more intentional. Third, you have to determine when it's time to sell or donate some of your objects entirely, if your space is filling up. Our feeling on this is, if it's something sentimental, ask yourself if the memory itself can somehow be enough for you, without having to keep the object. If it's something more aesthetic, put it in a closet for a month or two. If you don't miss it, that's probably all you need to know.

Styled shelves in the London home of Raphaël Zerbib

STYLING TIPS

Benjamin Reynaert

Before he was an independent New York creative director and stylist working on both interiors and commercial still lifes, Reynaert started his career sewing felt lobsters and bringing other craft projects to life for *Martha Stewart Living*. He's since styled the likes of Drew Barrymore's house (for *Domino* magazine) as well as campaigns for Farrow & Ball and One Kings Lane.

● Every room needs a bit of drama, and one of the easiest ways to achieve it is to fill a large floor vase with big branches clipped from your yard or street. I look for vases that are narrow at the top, wider in the middle, and tapered at the bottom. The narrow lip keeps the branches in place, and you can drop a rock inside for extra stability. Think of the styling in fifths: one-fifth for the vase, three-fifths for the branches, and one-fifth for the space between them and the ceiling.

● In addition to their usefulness in spotlighting a single object, pedestals or plinths can help fill empty corners and add extra vertical moments to a space. When you look around a room, it's important to have three to five of these different vertical moments—coffee table, side table, mantel, sideboard, etc.—so the eye doesn't get too stuck in one place.

● The real workhorse of coffee-table styling is a good tray placed underneath one or more objects. It instantly adds visual structure, and can make a group of incongruous objects that don't necessarily "match" suddenly feel related. Make sure you select a decent-size tray in relation to the size of your coffee table, so it doesn't get lost, and look for a contrasting color or material to create more visual interest.

● Dining tables can be difficult to style since they're so large. I like running a small collection of objects made from the same material down the center of a rectangular table, like five to seven (odd numbers are best) different glass vases. If you have a circular table, just cluster the same collection in the middle.

opposite: Sculptures by Alma Allen on a Brian Thoreen table in the Mexico City home of Su Wu

Hollister & Porter Hovey

Sisters and the cofounders of the Brooklyn home-staging firm Hovey Design,
Hollister and Porter have styled more than 400 apartments and houses for
the NYC real estate market, adding personality to a traditionally dull genre by
incorporating contemporary and vintage objects—plus Hollister's own colorful
paintings—into their much-Instagrammed interiors.

● On their own, what are referred to as "*jolie laide* colors"—putties, poopy browns, putrid yellows—can be hard to stomach, but when placed next to something very bright and saturated, or even neon, both colors will look better. And using one of those ugly/pretty shades will help super-colorful object collections feel grounded and calmer.

● We always insert art into our object vignettes, because paintings add visual interest and color pops that help give weight and context to the objects around them. But if you don't have an art collection, you can go DIY: Buy a canvas at an art store, paint it a single bright color, and place it behind a neutral-colored object to make that object stand out and add a sense of visual layering.

● Lamps don't always have to be practical; they can be used as objects themselves, or to highlight the objects around them. We love a pendant light hung incredibly low over an end table topped with a beautiful statue or a cluster of three items (one tall, one medium, and one short). For table lamps on consoles, we like the Laurel-and-Hardy-ish principle of pairing tall and skinny with short and round. Pair a short, chubby lamp with a tall, narrow object—or vice versa—and hang a painting three-quarters of the way toward the shorter object for visual balance.

● When styling large bookshelves, for visual balance, we recommend imagining the unit divided into a checkerboard pattern. Any objects you put into the "black squares" should be centered, while pieces on the "white squares" should alternate between being pushed to the left or pushed to the right. If we stack books horizontally in the center of one square, we'll put a few novels vertically to the left or right of the squares on either side. Then we add in the objects either on top of the book stacks or on their own. An object-laden bookcase will look better than books alone, and both need air and negative space.

● A few decorative objects in the bathroom can add warmth and interest in an otherwise cold and sterile setting. A stool can hold elegant bath items or flower-filled vases next to the tub; a craggy wooden one is nice, or you can use a ceramic garden stool for a bit of extra color, and for easy disinfecting.

opposite: The LA home of Jonathan Pessin

Tessa Watson

In addition to working as a stylist and art director for interiors and brands like 1stDibs, Hay, and Banana Republic, Watson also runs Øgaard, through which she provides visual inspiration and sources and sells artisanal objects, too.

● I like balancing natural materials with man-made pieces—contrasting the rough, irregular beauty of outdoor finds with the structure and perfection of machine-made objects. I've used large river rocks as doorstops and bookends, and I like putting wild, unruly branches in polished-metal vases. Or the opposite: adding precise, controlled arrangements to rough, hand-built clay vases.

● When you have a space that's not used regularly—like the top of a tall bookshelf—it makes sense to put objects there that you don't use regularly, either. I like to fill those spaces with collections that explore a theme, such as baskets, crystal, beautiful tools, or a certain type of ceramics. Groups of multiples add less visual clutter than groups of totally disparate items.

● Don't neglect the kitchen as a place for meaningful objects! Even if I'm acquiring a utility item for the kitchen that I already need, I try to find a beautiful, long-lasting version that I'll enjoy using, and enjoy looking at when it's not in use. I do this a lot when I'm traveling, seeking out tools or containers that have been historically produced in the area. I also love vintage kitchen tools, which I don't use but display like art.

● Don't be afraid to live with pieces in ways other than they were intended to be used. I once bought a platform bed frame from a woodworker and used it as a large coffee table. In my apartment in Mexico, I had a "stool" that I used for display and for extra seating that was actually a well-worn coconut-chopping pedestal I bought at a market. I also used a rippled clothes-washing board as a tray for displaying objects on the coffee table.

● Related: If you're constantly falling in love with—and buying—beautiful chairs, you can use them for something other than sitting. I love using mine as plant stands, and for displaying book stacks. The height that a chair seat offers a plant, or any other object, can give the eye a nice visual break between the floor and any table that might be in the room.

● If you have a piece of furniture that you need but don't like, buy several yards of a bold printed or woven fabric and drape it over the piece completely, all the way to the floor. It immediately brings the space a nice shock of color and texture. If you eventually find a better alternative for the piece, you can make the fabric into pillows, curtains, or tablecloths.

Katie Phillips

Phillips is a London-based stylist and set designer
specializing in interiors for commercial shoots including,
once, a four-story town house for a Burberry fragrance
shoot, inside which she helped build an entire London pub.

● Whenever I'm styling a vignette, I like to add an object that disrupts the scene around it—something that feels off-key and unexpected, to draw the eye and make visitors look twice. The trick is to make bold choices that feel intentional, and to only ever use one disruptive piece. For example, I have a collection of sculptural rocks on a shelf at home, among which I've carefully positioned a glossy yellow ceramic lemon. The gloss exaggerates the rawness of the rocks, while the hit of acidic color perfectly punctuates an otherwise monochrome moment.

● Plants add important visual and spatial impact to your home. When buying a plant—or placing it in a specific area—considering its color and shape is just as important as considering the color and shape of any other design object. A large plant with trailing vines and dark hues can be a dramatic counterbalance in a light space with a minimal aesthetic, while a small, vivid succulent with zigzag stems can help add height to a coffee table when placed atop a stack of books.

● Books can double as works of art in their own right. Leaned against the wall on a shelf to display their cover, or even literally framed and hung on the wall, a book can be as impactful as a painting. When stacking books on a coffee table, I save the ones with the most inspirational covers for the top. One tip is to always remove the dust jacket of a book to see what forgotten artwork might lie underneath—often the actual cover is more beautiful, and in better condition, too.

● Sitting in the center of the room, coffee tables can often be poorly lit, which means whatever you display on top of them will suffer, too. A great solution is to incorporate a lighting scheme into your styling, like a wireless lamp. The Flowerpot lamp by &Tradition is my favorite option for this—it's completely portable with a soft, atmospheric light.

● As coffee tables are usually within reaching distance, it's important to style them with pieces that can be picked up and handled. I always first consider how stable an object is, so a heavy-bottomed bowl or solid-brass paperweight will fare better than a tall, sculptural vase with a narrow foot. Opt for displaying pieces in hard-wearing materials such as wood or marble, and leave those made out of glass or porcelain for the higher-up shelves.

opposite: The London home of Tatjana Von Stein and Gayle Noonan

New York Living Rooms
Dominique Nabokov

The Modern Architecture of Cadaqués 1955-71

Logan Reulet

Based in Austin, Reulet got an MFA in painting but uses his formal training in composition for his work as a prop stylist and art director for commercial photo shoots—as well as for his own personal object still-life series, through which we discovered him on Instagram.

● Some objects are obvious showstoppers—don't visually diminish them by clustering them with other items. Give them room to shine. You can place a standout object on a pedestal or plinth, or on a smaller piece of furniture like a nightstand or side table. You can also use it to counterbalance a small grouping of objects on the opposite end of a mantel or a credenza.

● Risers are incredibly useful for adding height variation to a vignette, or adding visual weight to smaller objects. While a stack of books is always an option, they can sometimes add clutter to a space. Etsy has a large selection of risers in a variety of materials, often in customizable sizes. You can also get amazing deals at local stone or lumber yards on offcuts or discontinued samples.

● I like using candleholders to add visual variety to an object vignette. They add height and balance (when you have a pair), and you can find them in really interesting shapes and finishes. Whereas most objects tend to be shape-focused, candleholders are typically more linear, which helps break up a grouping that's getting too heavy.

● If a collection of objects has a strong common visual thread, it's easy to display them together. I focus on large or tall items first, then layer in smaller objects last. If the objects are mostly unrelated, though, layering can look too chaotic. Instead, arrange them in a more orderly fashion, with equal spacing between them. Cubby-style shelves also work great for this—providing separation that adds order to an eclectic mix of items.

● It's important to recognize how objects function visually within their environment when composing vignettes. A dark object will pop much more against a light wall, and vice versa, so if an object is standing out more than you'd like, move it to a less-contrasting environment.

● Styling in front of a window can be tricky. I stick to fewer objects with bold shapes and interesting silhouettes so that the objects aren't in competition with the view outside, and so they still have a presence even when they're backlit. Fewer objects will also keep your window more functional, of course, so you can still open it or use drapes.

At home with
CHARLOTTE TAYLOR

282

Taylor is an interior designer and art director best known for her collaborations with cutting-edge 3-D rendering talents around the globe, with whom she creates everything from fantasy homes to digital interiors and lookbook images for clients. Her London loft, which she shares with her partner, is filled with eBay finds, repurposed theater set-pieces, and the occasional fruits of her wood-whittling hobby.

" The Massimo and Lella Vignelli coffee table has to be one of my favorite design pieces I own. I included it in numerous rendered projects before it found its way into our apartment. A few pieces of furniture I use often in my digital homes have ended up in my home—it's lovely to finally have a tactile and physical relationship with them." →

"The white-stepped structures around my apartment are from an old theater set. They were originally two separate staircases painted in a garish faux-marble finish, but I repurposed them as decorative storage pieces. I love this method of displaying objects. The one in the living room was meant to be a stage for a record player. It makes you make a display out of it more, because it has this gallery feel to it."

"The stacked books around our apartment are actually more of a necessity than a design choice—I'm an avid researcher, so my book collection is ever-expanding and verges on hoarding. I use them on an almost daily basis, so it makes sense to have them easily accessible. I used to try to organize them by topic for easy referencing, putting all the bathroom books or all the living room books together, but that stopped after a while."

"I collected quite a few objects over the past year, with an emphasis on handmade, organic, and unusual pieces, predominantly in woods and metals. The ones on these shelves were all around the house before; a lot were on the dining table, and my partner said it was too much, so I built this makeshift shelf out of a few bricks and garden pavers. I got them at the local DIY store. I also use garden centers a lot, which is where I got all the rocks placed around the house, for two pounds each. I visually like them, and I think they offset the pieces I have that are quite polished and sharp." →

"Generally I like the bedroom to be pretty empty. We just have a few lamps and the stool in there most of the time. We like to use it as a room to sleep, and for it to be as calm as possible."

"I always loved mirrors. At home as a kid we had something ridiculous like thirty mirrors in the house, and more in the garden. I like the perspective and the light they add to a space. This one's from a gym—the big ones you find in a studio—and I found it on eBay. We had a similar-size mirror in our flat in Paris before, but that space was 250 square feet, so it really made a difference."

At home with

JOEY MEYERS & MARK BAEHSER

290

Vintage dealers **Meyers and Baehser**—who work under the name Ball and Claw and also cofounded the Brooklyn vintage co-op Dobbin St.—live in a 200-year-old Jersey City home, where they cycle favorite finds in and out and restyle them on the regular.

" The Baughman-style burl dining table helped jump-start this room, along with the Dancing Pendant light by Menu. We love oversized lighting since our rooms are larger, with high ceilings. The plaster console table moved around to a few different rooms before finding its home here. We love to move things around quite often in our house; most of the time when we find a piece we love, we bring it home with a place in mind but it winds up looking a million times better in a different place entirely." ↑

"We wanted our dressing room to have a moodier, Post-mod feel. The custom '80s arched floor mirror was a lucky estate-sale find. We're drawn to pieces with unique shapes, so we love how the mirror, drum pedestal, and chairs all work together—the story that mixing shapes and colors creates."

"We loved the old original details in this bathroom but wanted to add a modern touch without tackling any major renovations. We partnered with muralist and designer Liz Kamarul to create a custom abstract mural for the clawfoot tub. The bathroom fixtures were rescued from a home being torn down, and we painted them yellow. We also love the zephyr-style cantilever pedestal. It's perfect as a small table next to the tub."

66 Our Tito Agnoli chair is a piece that we knew we loved and had to find a place for. We stored it for more than a year before it found its final resting place in a corner of our bedroom. The art on the wall was also made by the same artist who made the wood lamp and side table in our office—we love carrying a story throughout different places in the house."

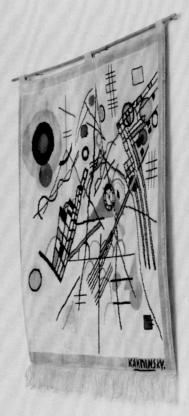

At home with

SADIE
PERRY

Perry is the London collector behind Mantel, the popular online purveyor of unusual vintage objects as well as artisanal ceramics sourced from Mexico. A former trend forecaster and jewelry designer, Perry also does interior styling and sourcing for private clients.

" One of my favorite objects I have is a 1930s Art Deco umbrella lamp. It really sums up my aesthetic, as I'm drawn to pieces that balance timeless elegance with an element of unexpected character or humor, giving them a strong presence in a room. I also gravitate towards pieces with unusual proportions or visibly handcrafted details that give them a human touch." ↑

"When I'm sourcing at markets or auctions, there might be pieces where I like the form but not the material or finish. I don't let that stop me from buying it if I see potential, because I can always sand and restain wood or paint metal. I painted this pair of black candle sconces a plaster-pink color to match my sofa and soften their bold shape. I've definitely fallen into the trap of thinking I'd get around to a project then realizing I'd taken on more than I bargained for, but simple changes are always worthwhile if you love an object and have a vision for it."

"I find that concentrating on a common color or material palette when styling collections anchors them and creates a more refined and cohesive look. I also like to soften the look of harder metal or glass pieces by placing them among contrasting textures or organic forms, like basketry or handcrafted pottery."

66 I've always been interested in the mantelpiece as the focal point in a room, and I've collected many inspiration images of people's curated mantels that I've found in books or online. It's a great way to display objects and artworks that express taste and character, especially because the architecture of the mantel itself is usually more interesting than that of, say, a plain shelf. You can continually change it up with new pieces, or pieces pulled from other areas of the house, without having to redecorate the room. The concept of my business was to offer people vintage objects that can be integrated into their homes, so naming it after the mantel I imagined them being displayed on helped give it context and meaning."

> "When I'm styling areas that are more functional, such as a dressing table, I like to include both decorative objects as well as functional ones. I also vary their heights and sizes while ensuring that there's at least one element of symmetry—a pair of matched candlesticks or two similar-size vases—to create balance." →

> "As my bedroom is quite small, I needed shelves up high to reduce my need for display furniture that would take up floor space. I have a lot of objects, and it's important to me to be able to have them on display, so this was a great solution." →

First and foremost, we must thank our agent, the indefatigable Kitty Cowles, who was the first person to help us understand—nay, demand!—that we had a book in us that needed to come out. As two people who never had a business plan for Sight Unseen, this was an unexpected but welcome detour. Thank you, Kitty, for cheerleading us, for being an incredibly wise sounding board, and for making this unfamiliar process as painless as possible. Never in a million years did we think we'd be spending that first pandemic summer writing a book proposal, but you made it happen.

To our editor, Angelin Borsics: Thank you for believing in this book from the beginning. From the very first call we had with you, it was clear that you—more than anyone else we spoke with—truly understood our vision, which was the motivation we needed to stay true to it from start to finish. You trusted us every step of the way, and you've been the best collaborator we could have dreamed of having the pleasure to work with on this project.

To our photographer, Charlie Schuck: This book would not be what it is without your unerring eye—and your framing of shots on an iPhone, our favorite new trick! Thank you for your creativity, your hard work, your flexibility, and your easy photographer banter, which helped our subjects feel more involved in the process. (Also thank you for your harebrained business schemes; we have so many ideas now for new Sight Unseen verticals.) Most of all, thank you for your ability to get the perfect shot, 100 percent of the time.

To our designer, Clémentine Berry of Twice Studio: Thank you for bringing such sophistication and taste to our beautiful design. You understood the aesthetic and overall vibe we were going for instantly. We love the details that make this book feel so very Sight Unseen.

To our art director, Mia Johnson: Thank you for your infinite patience—sorting through literally thousands of images with us, not raising an eyebrow when we wanted to change the color scheme for the tenth time, and letting us truly be involved in the process from start to finish. Your deft eye, your systemic thinking, your generosity, and your commitment made our vision for this book come alive.

To the rest of the team at Clarkson Potter, especially the crack marketing and publicity duo of Allison Renzulli and Jana Branson: Thank you so much for all your help bringing this book from a mere Google Doc to an actual thing out in the world! We're so excited to be part of the family.

To our impeccable stylists: Tessa Watson, we learned so much from traveling all over New York and Los Angeles with you—including that you can simply go out onto a Brooklyn street and snip a flowering branch to style a vase with?! Also, thanks to you, we will never again arrive at a photoshoot without a microfiber cloth in hand. It was so fun seeing these homes through your eyes. Thank you as well to Katie Phillips for having the foresight and professionalism to show up to all of our shoots in London with 50 pounds of art books and houseplants—and carry them up several flights of stairs—just to make absolutely sure you brought the magic (which you did).

Thank you to eBay, which not only helped make this book possible but also is probably the reason we know so much about vintage furniture and objects in the first place. The original inspo site.

Thank you to Mortlach Scotch Whisky for your tireless patronage of the design world and for making it possible for us to celebrate this book in style.

Thank you to Círculo Mexicano, whose Shaker-inspired rooms created a sense of calm during four hectic days in Mexico City. Thank you to Silverlake Pool & Inn and Ace Hotel Downtown Los Angeles for their hospitality—and their swimming pools.

Thank you to Rago/Wright in Chicago and to 1stDibs, which graciously allowed us to use so many photos from their incredible vintage catalogs.

Thank you so much to the subjects featured in this book, who allowed us to invade their homes, ransack their bookshelves, move their furniture around, and photograph the beautiful ways they've chosen to live.

Thank you to the many people who helped Sight Unseen become what it is today—without the support of our colleagues in the design world, and the inspiration of the many designers we've had the pleasure of featuring and collaborating with over the years, we would have never stuck with it long enough to grow this little hobby of ours into a global authority on great objects. Championing the work of young designers is something of our lives' mission, and you make it possible. And a special thank-you to Julie Lasky, who hired us both at *I.D.* magazine nearly twenty years ago, for being our first editor and champion—you are the reason we met, escaped the misogyny of corporate publishing, and created Sight Unseen in the first place.

Jill would like to thank her family and friends: Brad, who gave me, and always gives me, the time and space and support I needed to work on this project; Mom, Dad, and Emily for listening and being Sight Unseen's biggest fans; and Jonah and Isabel for their patience, good humor, and giggles. Thanks to my beloved Core 4, who provided me with music and friendship for, at minimum, two to four hours a day during the first year of putting together this book. Thanks to our Fanelli's chat, which provided a steady stream of memes, gossip, and other distractions, plus what feels like an eternity of encouragement. Thanks to Kelsey for always being a perfect authority on fonts (and everything else). And thanks to SP, who definitely always believed I was an authority on taste, ever since the days of the blue fleece.

Monica would like to thank: My family for being an unfailing support system and always answering my phone calls, and my friends for cheerleading and helping me stay excited about this book, even when I was so wrapped up in it I couldn't see beyond the edge of my laptop. Special thanks go to Nancy Einhart for the guestroom where I holed up for four days and wrote a large chunk of this book.

Lastly, we would like to thank the many readers and fans of Sight Unseen. We've been doing this for a long time, and there would be no point or value to what we do if not for those of you who have ever read a story, come to an exhibition, liked an Instagram post, bought an SU Friends membership, worn an Offsite tote, sent us a submission, linked to us on your blog (let's get old-school here), or simply told a friend how much you enjoy what we do. This book is for you.

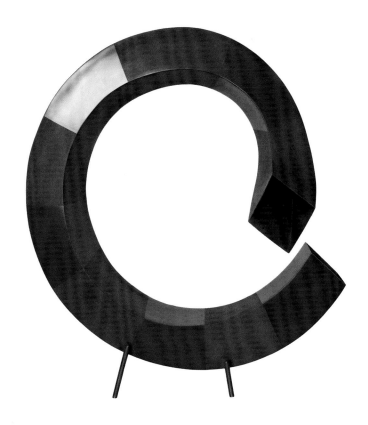

opposite: A bathroom lined in Marmoreal by Max Lamb for Dzek in the Los Angeles home of Yoram Heller and Eleanor Wells

above: Family of Form Gina Sculpture by Willem Van Hooff, 2020

Page numbers in *italics* refer to photographs and captions.

A

A1043 editions, *170*
A1043 gallery, 90
active objects, 21
Agnes Studio, *148*
Agnoli, Tito, *298*
AGO Projects, 148, *148, 152–153*
Akari, *247*
Albers, Anni, 36
Alhadeff, David, 95, 100, 112, 113, 115
Allen, Alma, 250, *251, 253, 272–273*
Alvarez, Anton, 95, 113, *166–167*
Anderson, CJ, *97*
&Tradition, 278
anonymous objects, 41
Anthologie Quartett, *40*
antiques, defined, 41
Aparicio, Attua, *165*
Apparatus, *130*
Appleton, Lora, *224–225*, 225, 269
Architectural Digest's "AD It Yourself," 177
Arranging Things, 102
Artemide, *246, 280–281*
Artigas, Carmen Cantu, *255*
artwork, object-like feel of, 21
Asahara, Shigeaki, 90, *90*
Astier de Villatte, *145*
Atelier de Troupe, 101
attributed objects, 41
Aulenti, Gae, 36, *56–57, 63*, 262, *262*

B

Bacon, Francis, 36
Baehser, Mark, *290–299*
Bakker, Aldo, *98*
Baldwin, Billy, 29
BaleFire, 167
Ball & Claw, 292
Barnes, Albert C., 25
Barnes, Elliot, *8*, 108, *110–111*, 139, *143, 145*, 269
Barovier, Angelo, *44–45*

Barovier & Toso, *44–45*
Barquet, Helena, *4–5*, 31, 50, 56, *118–127*
Barragán, Luis, 130
Beauget, Edouard, *3, 58-67*
beautiful objects, addiction to, 28
Belk, Russell W., 22-23
Bellini, Mario, 88
Bentley, Kathryn, *17, 230–239*
Bent Ply (Ngo), 88
Berger, Ueli and Susi, *80*
Bertoia, Harry, *28–29*
Bianco, Anthony, 170
Bi-Rite Studio, *8*
Bissell & Wilhite, *34*
Blauvelt, Andrew, 165, 176
Block Shop, 100
Bodmer-Turner, Simone, 167, *188*
Boeri, Cini, 36
Bogart, Seth, *80*
Bossy, Olivia, 25
Botta, Mario, *15, 280–281*
Bouterse, Harvey, *177*
Brand, Alex, *8*
Brandt, Marianne, 36
Braunschweiler, Marco Kane, *178*
Bredberg, Erika Kristofersson, *168–169*
Breuer, Marcel, 14
Brion Cemetery, 36
Brutalist movement, 36, 37
Buer, Peter, 210, *210*
Bukowski, Steven, 259
BZIPPY, 167, *175*

C

Calder, Alexander, 36, *37*
Calderone, Athena, 260
Campardo, Marco, *106*
Campbell, Abigail, 87
Cappello, Fabien, *148, 151, 152*
Carlberg, Helena, 170
Carpenters Workshop Gallery, 112
Carretero, Julien, *170*
Casa Ahorita, 102
Casa de Pilatos, *226*
Casa Shop, 41
Casabella magazine, 15
Cassina I Maestri Collection, 54
Castiglioni, Piero, *56–57*

CB2, 97, 112
Cedeño, Tomás Díaz, *134*
Charlap Hyman & Herrero, 80, *81*
Chen, Chen, 97, *101*, 106
Chiaozza, *154*
Chic by Accident, 130
Choplet, Nadeige, *20–21*
Cochran, Ian Alistair, *16*
Colantonio, F. Taylor, *125*
Cold Picnic, *123, 125*, 210
collectors' items, 86–91
Collins, Mac, *111*
Coming Soon, 50, 56, 120, *120*
Concrete Cat, *122, 125*
Confalonieri, Serena, *24*
Conran, Terence, 16
Constantine, Charles, *318*
contemporary objects, 92–161
  background, 94–97
  buying, 112–116
  defined, 95
  embracing discomfort, 156–161
  glimpse behind the curtain, 97
  at home with Barquet & Faria, *118–127*
  at home with Grattan, *128–135*
  at home with Primack & Weissenberg, *146–155*
  at home with Zerbib, *136–145*
  inspiration and, 100–102, *103–105*
  patronage and, 97
  shopping for, 106–108
Cool Machine, 61
Cranbrook Academy of Art, 107, 158
Cranbrook Art Museum, 165
Crespi, Gabriella, 36
Curated Spaces, 40, 51

D

Daguet, Christophe, *141*
Danese, *38*
de Beijer, Boris, *175*
de Cardenas, Rafael, 15
De Lucchi, Michele, *145*
Demory, Clarisse, 209, *209*
designer DIYs, 208–213
Dessecker, Bernhard, *53*
Directional, *37*
di Rossi, Pucci, *41*

Dims., 107
DIY Furniture and *DIY Furniture 2* (Stuart), 177
DIY projects
  by designers, 208–213
  instructions, 176–177, 274, *286*
Domino magazine, 177
Dowel Jones, *97*
Dream Collective, 232, *235*
Drijver, Peter, 177
Drobnis, Neal, *126*
Droog, 95
Duquette, Tony, 29
Dzek, *82*, 95, *313*
Dzekciorius, Brent, 95, 97, 115

E

Earnest Studio, *108–109*
Easy to Make Furniture, 177
East Fork Pottery, 167
Ecart International, *37*
Echo Park Pottery, 107
ED, *266*
Ede, Jim, 25
Egg Collective, 101, 112, *112–113*
Ekstrøm, Terje, *14*
Ellen's Next Great Designer (TV show), 130
Ellis, Aleisha, *168*
Ellwood, Craig, *76*
embracing discomfort, with contemporary
  objects, 156–161
Engman, Kjell, *222*
En la Mésá, 184
Ermičs, Germans, *92*
Etage Projects, 101, *113*
Evans, Paul, *37*
Everlund, Anna, *185*
Everybody.World, *84–85*
EWE studio, 130

F

Faria, Fabiana, *4–5*, 42, 50, *118–127*
Felton, Ian, *116*
Ferm Living, *116*
Ferreira, Roxanne, *108*
Fisher, Zoe, 107, 112, 116
@flex.mami, 177
Flos, 36
Fompeyrine, Bertrand, *134*
Fontana Arte, *56–57*
Fornasetti, *80*
Fort Standard, 112, 226
Fowler, Eve, *232*
Franck, Josef, *84–85*
Franck, Kaj, 170
Frankel, Robbie, *162*, 167
Fredericks and Mae, *127*
French industrial design, 71
Friedman Benda, 24, 97, 101, 106, *107*, 269
Fritz Hansen, 107
Future Perfect, The, 95, 101, *101*, *167*,
  174–175

G

Gallacher, Jermaine, 101
Garmentory, 102
Garza, José Pérez, *252*
Gerstley, Sean, *8*, 167, *181*
Giacometti, Alberto, 56
gifts, 226–227
Gilbert, Alex, 24, 41, 42, 97, 107, 108,
  115, 116, 269, 270
Giraud, Pierre Marie, *172*
Glas Italia, *114–115*
Gordon, Beverly, 219
Graham, Elyse, 170, *175*
Grattan, Mark, *10–11*, *13*, *128–135*
Gray, Eileen, 36, *37*
Green River Project, 112
Griffin, Cassie, *122*
Gross, Barbara, *224–225*
Guzzini, Harvey, *266*

H

Halmos, Jeff, *12–13*, *190–199*
handmade objects, 162–213
  background, 164–165
  brief history of, 165–167
  buying, 171–173
  designer DIYs, 208–213
  at home with Kim, *200–207*
  at home with Mayock & Halmos,
    190–199
  at home with Mupangilaï, *182–189*
  making, 176–177
  new luxury of, 170
  rehabbing, 180–181
  rise of studio objects, 167–170
Hartley, Joe, *180*
Harvard, Ceramics Program, 107
Haulenbeek, Steven, 173, *173*
Hay, 94, *98*, 102, 106, 107, 108,
  170
Heinze, Kelsey, *56*, *221*
heirlooms, 225
Held, Mark, *84–85*
Heller, 85
Heller, Yoram, *30*, *78–85*,
  276–277, *313*
Hem, 106
Hennessey, James, 177
Herman Miller Chiclet
  sofa, 15, *64*
Herman Miller Company
  Store and outlets, 108
Herrera, Natalie, 167
Hjorth, Axel Einar, 35
Hoffmann, Josef, 36, *37*,
  217
Hogan, John, *167*, 170
Holz, Jochen, 170,
  174–175
The House Book (Conran),
  16

Hovey, Hollister & Porter, 274
Hovey Design, 274
How to Construct Rietveld Furniture (Drijver),
  177
Hoyt, Cody, *8*, *171–172*, *236–237*
Hughes, Andrew O., 167
The Hunt (Parrish), 40

I

Ikea, 15, *16*
Iko Iko, *234*
Instant Furniture (Stamberg), 177
Italian design, 36, *37*
Iturbide, Graciela, *254*

J

Jacobsen, Sophie Lou, 170
Jardín, *255*
Johnson, Casey, 167
Johnston, Doug, 170
Jorgensen, C., *222*
Judd, Donald, 176, 269

K

Kahn, Misha, 106, *107*, 263
Kamarul, Liz, *297*
Kaplan, Danny, *186*
Karakter, *98*
Kardana, M., *38–39*
KASSL, 106
Khemsurov, Monica, 14, 25, 31, 55, 108,
  112, 217, *217*, *218*, 219, 220, *220*, *222*,
  225, *227*
Kim, Minjae, *200–207*

Kim, Pat, 213, *213*
Kim, Sang Hoon, 160, *160*
Klug, Ubald, *82*
Knoll, 107, 108
Kohlmann, Emma, *232*
Kollekted By, 102
Kondo, Marie, 271
Kosta Boda, *222*
Kruger, Barbara, 225
Krzykowski, Matylda, 22, 25, 265
Kuramata, Shiro, *52–53*, 246

L

Lacombe, Rémi, *82*
Ladies & Gentlemen Studio, 177
Lagerfeld, Karl, 15
Laing, Gerald, *44*
Lalese Stamps, *176*
Lamb, Max, *82*, 115, *178–179*, *313*
Lanza Atelier, *153*
Laposse, Fernando, *154*
Larson, Annie Lee, 180
Lee, Jennie Jieun, *236*
Lee, MyoungAe, *205*
Levi, Helen, 167
Lewinger, Forrest, 167, 212, *212*
Li, Lykke, 262
Lindner, Richard, *82*
Lock, Catherine, 25, 164
Loft and Thought, *186*
Lollar, Karen, 22
Loose Parts, 177
lost-wax casting, *173*
Love House, *62*, 101
Lukin, Anna, 170

M

Mach, Peggy, *260*
Mackintosh, Charles Rennie, *54*
Magistretti, Vico, 36
Magliaro, Joseph, 15
M.A.H Gallery, *168*
Male Glaze, *80*
Malouin, Philippe, *100*
Maniera, *111*
Mantel, 302
Marcelis, Sabine, *103*, 106
Mardahl, Helle, 170
Mari, Enzo, *38*, 176
Marigold, Peter, 177
Marimekko, 14, 31
Mario Tsai Studio, *94–95*
Markos, Stephen, 90
Marmoreal, *82*
Marstaller, Lukas, *168*
Marx, Roberto Burle, 36
mass appeal of design, 15–16
Mass Modern auction, 108
Matter, 101
Maurer, Ingo, *22, 53*
Maus, Susanne, *53*

maximalism, 25
Mayock, Lisa, *12–13*, *190–199*
McMahon, Elise, 176–177
Mdina, *61*
Melake, Luam, *104–105*
Melgaard, Bjarne, 159
Memor Studio, 167, *178*
Memphis design movement, 31, 36, *139*,
    142, *151*, 259, *293*
Memphis Group, 95
Mendini, Alessandro, 15, *34*
Menu, *292*
Merci, 102
Mexican Majolica, *152*
Meyers, Joey, *290–299*
Meyers, John, 24, 49
Meyers, Linda, 49, 268, 271
Meyers, Zesty, 165
Michelsen, Roberto, *255*
Mid-Century Modern Furniture Refinishing
    Resource, The, 181
Midtbo, Maxine, 167
Mies van der Rohe, Ludwig, *76*
Mihich, Vasa, *222*
minimalism, 25, *149*
Modern House, The (blog), 25, 269
Modernism movement, 25, 41
modern objects, 41
Modern Times, 101
MoMA Design Store, 102
Monologue, 101
Moore, Emi, 41
Morga, Gary, *145*
Morris, Tom, 269
Moser, Koloman, 36
Mosqueda, Juan, 97
Mosser, *123*
Mr. Goodbar, 71, *72*
Muecke, Jonathan, 20, 158, *158*
Mulholland, Martha, *214*, *226*
Muller Van Severen, *103*, 106
Mupangilaï, Kim, *5*, *182–189*
Murano Glass, *32*, *38*, 170
Muuto, 108, *108–109*

N

Nagel, Andrés, *43*
Nalle, Charles, 87, *87*
Nash, Carmen, 48, *186*
nerikomi, *171*
The New Craftsmen, 25, *111*, 164,
    180
New York magazine, 15, 167, 176
New York Times, 16
Newell, Pip, 40, 51, 56
Newson, Marc, 115
Ngo, Dung, 88, *254*
Nichols, Isaac, 167
Nicola L, *30*, *82*
Nielson, Mariah, 217
Nilsson, Jonatan, 102, *228–229*
Nilufar Gallery, *23*, *98–99*

Nizzoli, Marcello, 88
Nomadic Furniture (Hennessey & Papanek),
    177
Noonan, Gayle, *240–247*, *278–279*, *280–281*
Not For Sale, 71, *71*, *72*, *76*

O

objects
    contemporary, 92–161. *See also*
        contemporary objects
    handmade, 162–213. *See also* handmade
        objects
    sentimental, 214–265. *See also*
        sentimental objects
    styling of, 266–309. *See also* styling
    understanding, 21–25. *See also*
        understanding objects
    vintage, 26–91. *See also* vintage objects
Odd Matter, *23*, *98–99*
The Ode To, *168–169*, 170, *170*
Okuda, Shin, *234*, 235
Olinet, Vincent, *252*
Olivetti typewriters, 88
Olunkwa, Emmanuel, 211, *211*
Olympic torch (Shire), *74–75*
Opening Ceremony, 15
Oppenheim, Méret, 36
Orbernai, F., *46–47*
originality, of vintage objects, 28
originals, 42
Osgerby, Barber, *114–115*
Ottenberg, Mel, 264
Otto, Haus, *117*

P

Panton, Verner, *16*
Papanek, Victor, 177
Parker, Eny Lee, 95, 167
Park Pardon, *218*

Amphora by F. Taylor Colantonio, 2018

Parrish, Patrick, 29, 40, 47, 55, 56
Pasmore, Victor, *246*
passive objects, 21
Patrick Parrish Gallery, *104*
Paulsen, Fredrik, *113*
Peck, Morgan, *236–237*
Perriand, Charlotte, 16, *71*
Perry, Sadie, *32*, 222–223, *300–309*
Pesce, Gaetano, 95, *113*, 155
Pessin, Jonathan, *68–77*, *274–275*
Phillips, Katie, 278
Picasso, Pablo, *53*
plywood furniture, 88
polyester yarn, 161
polyurethane foam, 160
Pong, Ellen, 157, *157*
Ponti, Gio, 36, 88, *88*
Primack, Rodman, *146–155*
Prip, John, *44*
Prisunic, *84–85*
Prouvé, Jean, 15–16, *71*
provenance, 15. *See also* vintage objects

Q

Quasimodo Chair, *40*

R

R & Company, *104–105*, 165
Radical Architecture movement, 36
Rebelo, Hélène, *3, 5, 58–67*
reeditions (reproductions), 42
Reform Kitchens, 106
Reid, Hilary, 176
Restoration Hardware Cloud Sofa, *235*
Reulet, Logan, 281
Rey, Michael, *251*
Reyes, Charlyn, *185*
Reyes | Finn, *115*
Reynaert, Benjamin, 273
Rezek, Ron, *253*
Richoz, Julie, 170
Richter, Keren, 180, 181
RISD, 159
Risley, John, *80*
Roll & Hill, 101
Rogen, Seth, 167
Roman, Alison, 167, 261
Rowley, Aviva, 216, *216–217*, 222
RP Miller, 148
RW Guild, 102
Ryan, Kathleen, *251*

S

Salon 94 Design, *100, 113, 178–179*
Sangyo, Koyo, *259*
Saporiti, 36
Scarpa, Afra, 36
Scarpa, Carlo, 170
Scarpa, Tobia, 180
Schanck, Chris, 95, *115*

Scheid, David, *80*
Schenk-Mischke, Philipp, *103*, 113
Schumacher, *80*
SEEDS Gallery, 101, *165*
Selim-Boualam, Oliver, *168*
Sella Concept, 243
Sella Studio, *244*
sentimental objects, 214–265
    background, 216–217
    favorite things, 258–265
    gifts, 226–227
    heirlooms, 225
    at home, 228
    at home with Bentley, *230–239*
    at home with Von Stein & Noonan,
        240–247
    at home with Wu, *248–257*
    primal connections, 217
    souvenirs, 219–221
    stories, not styles, 218
Serruys, Thomas, *186*
Shamshiri, Pamela, 235
Shaw, James, 24, *104*
Shire, Peter, *17, 74–75*, 95, 107, *232–233,
    236–237*
SHOP Cooper Hewitt, 102
Side Gallery, 101
Sight Unseen
    Artist's Proof column, 208
    At Home With column, 15
    founding, 15
    mission of, 14–15, 22, 97
Sight Unseen Offsite, 16
Simms, Sally, 89
Simons, Raf, *155*
Singer, Fanny, 217, 219, 221
Singer, Jill, 14, 102, 112, 116, 165, 217,
    220, 222, 225, *228–229*
Sirius Glassworks, *220*
Sister Parish, 29
Smeulders, Tijmen, 161, *161*
social media, 15–16, 35, 40, 107, 116, 167,
    177, 181, 216
Soft Baroque, *104*
Sottsass, Ettore, *80*, 82, 88, *264, 264,
    276–277*
Souvenir, The: Messenger of the Extraordinary
    (Gordon), 219
souvenirs, 219–221
Sowden, George, 94
Spartan Shop, 101
Spazio Nobile Gallery, *102–103*
SSENSE, 15
Stacey, George, 29
Stamberg, Peter, 177
Starck, Philippe, *56*
Stewart, Sam, *111*, 116
Stockman, Lily and Hopie, 100
Stout, Katie, *125*, 159, *159*, 167
Stuart, Christopher, 177
Studio Anansi, *178*
Studio Anne Holtrop, *111*
Studio IMA, TK

Studio POA, *98*, 113
Study O Portable, 97
styling, 266–309
    background, 268
    basic styling principles, 269–271
    defined, 268
    at home with Ball and Claw Vintage,
        290–299
    at home with Perry, *300–309*
    at home with Taylor, *282–289*
    styling tips, 273–281
Sukrachand, Robert, 97
Sung, Phoebe, 210, *210*
Superhouse, *181*
Svatun, Falke, *18*
Swedish Grace movement, 35

T

Takagi, Jonah, 116, 170
Taylor, Charlotte, *266*, *282–289*
Taylor, Gerard, *40*
Tessier, Jason, *145*
The Future Perfect, 95, 101, *101*, *167,
    174–175*
The New Craftsmen, 25, *111*, 164, *180*
The Ode To, *168–169*, 170, *170*
Third Drawer Down, *121*
@thishouse5000, 177
Thomas, Rachel, *168*
Thonet, *217*
Thoreen, Brian, *253*, *272–273*
Tieghi-Walker, Alex, 219
Toogood, Faye, *104*, 106
Tribu Editions, *34*
trompe l'oeil, *82*

U

understanding objects, 20–25
    background, 20
    how to live with objects, 24–25
    what is an object? 21
    why we live with objects, 22–23

V

Valat, E., *32–33*
Valerie Objects, 106
van de Gruiter, Jeroen, *227*
Van Dusen, Ellen, 176, 180, 259
Van Eijk, Kiki, *102–103*
Van Hooff, Willem, *313*
Varier Furniture, 14
Vev Viganò, *228*
Vignelli, Lella, *284–285*
Vignelli, Massimo, *37*, *284–285*
Villa Necchi Campiglio, 36
vintage objects, 26–91
    background, 28
    buying, 54–56
    collectors' items, 86–91
    defined, 41

vintage objects (*cont.*)
  at home with Heller & Wells, *78–85*
  at home with Pessin, *68–77*
  at home with Rebelo, *58–67*
  inspiration and, 35–36, *37–39*
  mystery and history of, 29–31
  permission to let loose, 31, *32–34*
  shopping for, 40–42, *43–46*
  shopping guides, 47–51
  why now? 29
Vitra, 107, *276–277*
Volume Gallery, 101, *172*
Vonnegut / Kraft, 112
von Stein, Tatjana, *240–247, 278–279, 280–281*
Vreeland, Diana, 28

W

Waka Waka, 112, *234, 235*
Walrod, Jim, *82,* 90, 264
Wang & Söderström, *98,* 113
Wary Meyers, 24, 49, 198, 268
Watson, Tessa, 277
Wearstler, Kelly, 28, 40
Weil, Daniel, *40*
Weinberger, Natalie, *96–97,* 167
Weissenberg, Rudy, *146–155*
"well-resolved" objects, 21
Wells, Eleanor, *30,* 78–85, *276–277, 313*
West Elm, 97
Westman, Gustaf, *62*
White Arrow, 180
@whydidyoupaintthat, 181
Wiener Werkstätte, 36, *37*
Wilhite, Robert, *34*
Williams, Kai, 97, *101,* 106
Wolfe, Thaddeus, 170, *172–173*
Workaday Handmade, 167, 212
Wright auction house, 108
Wright Now, 108
Wu, Su, 217, 221, 226–227, 228, *248–257, 270, 272–273*

Y

YOWIE, 102

Z

Zanoth, Wilhelm, *22*
Zarbock, Karol, *170*
Zaven, *164–165*
Zerbib, Raphaël, *1–2, 5, 8, 136–145, 269, 271*
Ziff, Toby, 91
Ziperstein, Bari, 232, *236–237*

Magna Chair by Charles Constantine for Sight
Unseen x Bestcase, 2022

MONICA KHEMSUROV and **JILL SINGER** are cofounders of the online magazine *Sight Unseen*, one of the most influential design publications in the United States. Former editors of *I.D.* magazine, they also work as freelance writers, curators, and consultants. Khemsurov is a contributing editor for *T: The New York Times Style Magazine* and a contributor to *Bon Appétit*, *Bloomberg Businessweek*, and *W*, while Singer's writing has appeared in *PIN–UP*, *Elle Décor*, *T: The New York Times Style Magazine*, *W*, and more. Both live and work in New York City.

Copyright © 2022 by Monica Khemsurov and Jill Singer
Photographs © 2022 by Charlie Schuck

All rights reserved.
Published in the United States by Clarkson Potter/
Publishers, an imprint of Random House, a
division of Penguin Random House LLC,
New York. clarksonpotter.com

CLARKSON POTTER is a
trademark and POTTER with
colophon is a registered
trademark of Penguin Random
House LLC.

Library of Congress
Cataloging-in-Publication Data
is available.

ISBN 978-0-593-23504-1

Printed in China

Editor: Angelin Borsics
Editorial assistant: Darian Keels
Designers: Mia Johnson and Twice Studio
Production editor: Mark McCauslin
Production manager: Kim Tyner
Compositors: Merri Ann Morrell, Nick Patton, and Hannah Hunt
Copy editor: Andrea Peabbles

Indexer: Jay Kreider
Marketers: Allison Renzulli and Windy Dorresteyn
Publicist: Jana Branson

10 9 8 7 6 5 4 3 2 1

First Edition

The Brooklyn home of Kim Mupangilaï